Atlas America

After Default, Will Atlas Shrug?

A State Ratified Federal Limit Amendment? A 3rd Party? Steps to Constitutional Federal Government?

By: B. J. Galt

Copyright

For printed copies of this book:
https://www.createspace.com

Atlas America

Title ID: 4064790

Also on Kindle & at Amazon Books

ISBN-13 978-1481049306

ISBN-10 1481049305

Email request a Free book PDF from
B. J. Galt Email: bjongalt@gmail.com

PREFACE: ATLAS AMERICA

Constitutional America?

America represents a unique, shining example in government. Its success is the envy of people all over the world. The governmental concepts of freedom as defined in the US Constitution create powerful forces that generate unprecedented economic prosperity that is far greater than any other nation.

American GDP is greater than China, Japan, the UK and Germany combined. Many countries depend on America for economic, charitable and military support. America is truly Atlas to the World! When faced with a

$ Multi -Trillion, unsustainable, national debt;

Will Atlas be forced to shrug?

A State Ratified Federal Limit Amendment? A 3rd Party? Steps to Constitutional Federal Government?

PARTS

PART I

AMERICA IS ATLAS TO THE WORLD

America represents a unique, shining example in government. Its success is the envy of people all over the world. Its history is proof that "freedom to pursue happiness" is a powerful incentive. This simple, government concept defined in the US Constitution is a powerful force that generates unprecedented economic prosperity that is far greater than any other nation.

This country in a period of 230+ years has risen to such heights as to possess over 60 percent of the world's wealth while having only about 7 percent of the world's population? The economy of the United States is greater than the economies of Japan, Germany, China, the United Kingdom and France **combined.**

As a result of this unprecedented success, many countries depend on America for military, economic and charitable support.

Where in the world is our Military?   On 700+ bases in 135 nations.   .

Consider the industry,   logistics, facilities and equipment costs to support the Military Complex. The proposed 2015 Federal Military Budget is $610 Billion. The United States spends more on its military than any other nation in the world. The United States military budget accounts for almost 45% of the world's military spending. Its defense budget is nearly six times larger than that of China, even though China's army is almost double the size of the United States.

President Eisenhower, as he was leaving office, warned; "Beware of the Military Industrial Complex".

America is truly Atlas to the World! Will it be possible for America to continue in this role without threatening its future?

The 2015 $3.8 Trillion Federal Budget with a projected $438 Billion deficit clearly indicates a Federal Government that is fiscally out of control.

Future unfunded liabilities in Social Security and Medicare and the new Health Reform Bill will continually add to the Federal debt creating fiscal conditions that threaten insolvency and the survival of the United States of America.

Will Atlas America be forced to shrug?

What is needed is **Recurrence to Fundamental Principles**" which is periodically essential to the maintenance of a free society. This book will present the example of a new Federalist check and balance; a State ratified "Federal Limit Amendment". Also >40 initiatives are proposed to reestablish truly constitutional operation of the Federal Government. The need for a 3rd party is *al*so considered.

PART II

THE PROBLEM: EXCESSIVE GOVERNMENT

America today is facing an internal danger that is far greater than any external threat posed by any hostile nation. It is a corrosive, deadly danger. If left unchecked, it will certainly cause the downfall of this great nation. It is difficult in this age of an "affluent society", where "instant gratification" is prevalent, to believe that such an eventual downfall could occur. But the lessons of human history have clearly proven that it surely will happen unless our course is changed. This is not some far off danger. It is quite possible that we who are living today may witness the end of the American dream of freedom for the individual and "government of the people, by the people and for the people".

CORRUPTIVE BIG GOVERNMENT

<u>The 2015 $3.8 Trillion Federal Budget is simply too large to be effectively managed.</u> Even worse, these massive funds and the related federal powers they represent corrupt federal representative politicians and bureaucrats. This was clearly demonstrated when the Republicans came to control the Presidency and the legislative

branches with majorities. Access to all that money and power turned them into fiscally irresponsible spenders

President Bush added to the problem by never vetoing any Republican spending bill. He authorized the Iraq and Afghanistan wars, the Part D Medication program, the Economic Stimulus Act of 2008 and the TARP bank bailout, all without budgetary funding, thereby allowing unprecedented deficits to be created.

When the Republicans succumbed to these attractions, they lost their reputation as the party of constitutional, economic small government and low taxes and thereby they lost the Conservative faithful. Republicans did not change government, government changed the party. The question for the Republicans now is, can they reestablish their previous reputation in a believable way?

In the first year of the Obama administration, the expansion of government was on steroids. Using the Democratic congressional majorities and Presidency the $800 Billion American Recovery and Reinvestment Act of 2009 was passed to stimulate the economy. Mostly it has used to stimulate and grow the Federal Government. It has failed to effectively improve the unemployment conditions. Its main effect has been to expand the number of Federal employees and bolster state budgets. So it is not surprising that this massive government directed spending had little effect in improving the recession and related private sector job prospects.

Bailout funding of General Motors and Chrysler extended Federal power into the private sector as never before seen.

The Obama administration and Democratic congressional majority also passed the 2500 page Affordable Care Act (Obama Care) with future implications of massive increases in Federal controls, bureaucracies and related costs.

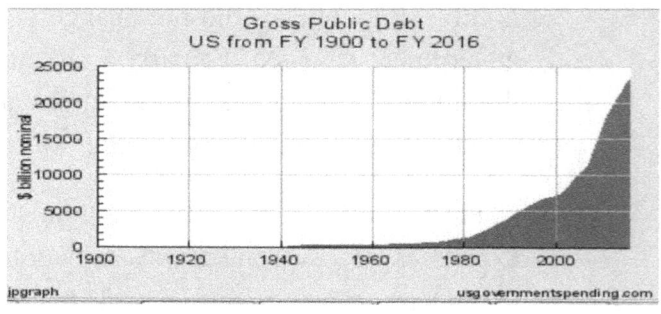

The 2015 Federal debt is $18+ Trillion. Continuing Deficit spending adds to the debt every year. Insolvency due to growing debt interest payments is a real possibility. Neither party proposes balanced budgets . What will we pass on to our grandchildren; unfillable program promises, massive, uncontrollable government and unsustainable national debts?

All of the budget plans proposed by the Democrats or Republicans only address reducing the budget deficit (spending over a balanced budget). <u>These plans only reduce the amount of budget growth.</u> Small reductions are made over a 10 year period. No meaningful cuts are made now. These plans require that future legislators must do the actual cutting to reduce possible budget growth.

None of the plans actually reduce the $18+ Trillion current national debt. How long can this go on before funding realities will force insolvency? How will our children deal with these generational debt burdens?

GOVERNMENT TOO BIG TO SURVIVE?

We hear that some financial and auto companies are too big to be allowed to fail because, if they fail, there will be national and international catastrophic, systemic effects. It is actually possible that they are too big to survive. The same can be said of the Federal Government with its enormous size, management structures, operational duplication, inefficiencies and future debt potentials.

We have had the Tech Bubble, the Housing Bubble, now we have the Government Bubble. By their nature, bubbles are always temporary and then they burst. The Government Bubble is more like a balloon. But it too has expansion limits beyond which it will burst. Limit control is essential for survival.

The **Peter Principle** is the principle that "In a bureaucracy, everyone tends to rise to their level of incompetence". Formulated by Dr. Lawrence Peter in his 1968 book *"The Peter Principle"*. This principle has real validity. It holds that in a bureaucracy of government or business, members are promoted so long as they work competently. Sooner or later they are promoted to a position at which they are no longer competent (their "level of incompetence"), and there they remain.

Peter's corollary states that <u>"in time, every post tends to be occupied by an employee who is incompetent to carry out his duties"</u> and adds that "work is then accomplished by those employees who have not yet reached their level of incompetence".

This principle and problem is very true in government as well as private sector bureaucracies. In fact, the problem is made worse by the difficulty in eliminating unionized, incompetent government workers as well as the tendencies of government departments to perpetually expand. These departments will always ensure that their budgets are fully spent so they will not be reduced, and they will promote efforts to justify their expansion in the next budget cycle.

The evolution and expansion of Social Security, Medicare and Medicaid illustrate the truth of these principles. Not only have they been expanded to levels of mismanagement, the trust funds intended to effectively fund these programs have been raided, transferring their funds to general spending programs. So now these programs are in jeopardy of inadequate funding and in need of major reforms to keep them solvent. Both parties are reluctant to address these reform needs because of the political implications of having to reduce or significantly change the programs and then deal with the related reactions from the program beneficiaries.

The Affordable Care Act (Obama Care) further expands the role of the Federal Government to even higher levels of economic and health care involvement. The examples of its passage and start up illustrate how inept and incompetent massive bureaucracies can be.

To the size of a state there is a limit, as there is to plants, animals and implements, for they can none of them retain their facility when they are too large.

Aristotle

Loss of Governmental Control

The danger for America is that of the people losing control of their government and the directly related effect; the creation of excessive, inefficient, burdensome, character-crushing government. This danger is already extensive in its implementation and it is capable of exponentially increasing its growth rate in proportion to the degree of its prevalence. This is especially true about the Federal Government. State governments have also grown proportionally and have similar entrenched personnel problems. But they represent a lesser danger because they are more subject to local control and many have constitutional requirements to meet balanced budget requirements.

Voters see representatives who disregard their election promises once elected and are too influenced by lobbyists and political pressures.

Most youths have no faith that Social Security benefits will be there when they need them. Projections indicate that they are well justified in these beliefs. The Social Security System has been receiving more than is paid out for many years. However these surpluses were not allowed to accumulate in a Trust Fund as authorized thereby creating a well financed system. Instead the Congress has used and continues to use the surpluses for general budget expenses and provides IOU's to the Social Security trust accounts for these funds. With the Federal budget running deficits and expanding debt, these IOU's are meaningless in value.

How can this be? How can this great people, possessed of such literacy and the best communications that technology can provide be in danger of losing control of their government? The answer is simply that the government has become too large to be effectively controlled through elected representatives. Today, constitutionally defined checks and balances have been bypassed or made ineffective. President Obama uses Executive Orders to override or modify existing laws. The main error is in the abandonment of the constitutionally defined roles of State and Federal Government. The Federal Government, by virtue of its remote and extensive nature, presents by far the greatest present problem of control for the people. Its size exceeds the ability of the people and their representatives to effectively comprehend its complexity and intelligently, democratically control it.

REPRESENTATIVE CONTROL

We expect to control our government at the federal level through our representatives, but this assumes that our representatives, in turn, truly can have control when elected. These lines of control seem extremely fragile when we consider that each of us can only vote for one senator and a congressional representative with each election. There are totals of 100 senators and 537 representatives who must control close to 3,000,000 federal employees and manage a $3.8 Trillion budget. The mind boggles at such expectations, especially if one recognizes that most of these representatives' time is spent in the proposing and processing of new legislation and in raising money and working to be re-elected.

Your money is spent through massive Appropriations Bills developed and promoted by lobbyists, passed by the Congress and signed by the President. The Government does not have any money. Through taxes, it takes money from you and borrows and prints more, then spends that! The Iraq and Afghanistan wars, the Part D Prescription Drug programs and The bailouts of 2008 and 2009 were all done with deficit spending. The Federal Debt in 2015 is $18+ Trillion. This is a debt that will burden future generations and can never be eliminated with taxation. As the Federal Reserve monetizes the debt by printing money, the dollar is devalued ultimately leading to hyper-inflation.

Expect to see continuing deficits in the foreseeable future, leading to much more debt. **Interest payments on that debt will become the largest item in the federal budget**.

Congressional oversight of government operations is not a major priority. Oversight is usually driven by political expediency or only in the case of gross discrepancies or corruption. If oversight does uncover ineffective operations that should be terminated, Congress is reluctant to do so due to the pressures from those receiving services from such operations and their lobbyists.

It would be accurate to say that this form of government is, in truth, more bureaucratic than representative. The fact that Congress is no longer reflecting public opinion was illustrated by the way the 2500+ page Affordable Care Act (Obama Care) was passed with little transparency, vote bribery and only Democrat party support.

Most people do not have a real sense of how much money and massive power a $3.8+ Trillion Federal Budget represents. Their minds cannot truly comprehend such large numbers. Along with the lobbyists, the special interests and entrenched bureaucracy involved, all this power and money has the potential to overwhelm and corrupt the best intentioned politicians.

GOVERNMENT - A DANGEROUS FORCE

Citizens are beginning to sense the truth of what George Washington said many years ago:

"Government is not reason, it is not eloquence. It is a force. Like fire, it is a dangerous servant and a fearful master".

The government, unless it can be made effectively responsive to the desires of the people, will continue to be an ever-growing force that will ultimately attain burdensome mastery over a dependent people and thereby cause the corruption and erosion of their character and strength. It is these latter effects on character that will ultimately cause the downfall of the nation.

This pattern of national degradation is not new to mankind. There is an abundance of historical and present examples. Examine the nations of the world, especially those in the European area that have intensively developed systems of socialistic government but still claim to be part of the free world. The individuals in such nations are frustrated and submerged under the smothering influences of governmental controls and heavy tax burdens. These nations have passed their peaks and are definitely in states of decline.

British MP Daniel Hannan in his book "The Plan" describes the effects of excessive Socialist government in the United Kingdom:

"The state has become so large and unwieldy, the number of officials benefiting from the status quo so great, that no single minister, be he the most energetic in Whitehall, can refashion it. So what is going wrong? Why does the state fail? The answer is that modern government is already running at capacity. It has taken too much on. It is literally unable to assume new functions and discharge them efficiently."

"As Kenneth Boulding put it: 'The larger and more authoritarian the organization, the better the chance that its top decision-makers will be operating in purely imaginary worlds'.

Friedrich Hayek, in his 1944 economic treatise, "The Road to Serfdom", Hayek could see that centralization was unsuited to the complexities of modern administration.

MP Hannan's Plan proposed a 12-month legislative programme that is based on these three principles:

Decisions should be taken as closely as possible to the people who are affected by them.

Decision-makers should be directly accountable.

The citizen should be as free as possible from state coercion.

Prime Minister Margaret Thatcher, the most conservative of Britain's leaders said, "The problem with Socialism is that you run out of other people's money."

We in America would be wise to study Britain's example and to relate it to developments in our country.

THE ROMAN EMPIRE

The old Republic Aerarium (Congressional equivalent) became merely a municipal treasury. The officers of the Emperor's body guard became the great officers of the state. His private council became the supreme court of appeal. All power resided in him and he was looked to for all provisions. This centralized power caused a paralysis of effective administration, with a related corruption of officials at all levels. Municipal liberty was lost and with this came evil, repressive fiscal systems that caused the decay of the middle classes. Once this core strength was destroyed, complete disorganization set in, which facilitated the dismemberment of the empire and its eventual collapse.

THE GREEK EMPIRE

The same general pattern can be seen in the history of the Greek Empire. Its eventual collapse too can be traced to a decay of public spirit which led to corruption in public life and government.

Edith Hamilton wrote this about the decline of Athens; *"When the freedom they wished for most was freedom from responsibility, then Athens ceased to be free and was never free again."*

TToday, Greece is considered to be near bankruptcy requiring repeated bail outs to support operations having allowed its government to far exceed the capacity of its people to support it.

OTHER EXAMPLES

A "Life Line" article had this to say about patterns of national decay: *"The pages of history tell the story of twenty nations which have been free. Their average length of life has been just two centuries, two hundred years. The cycle has been plain to see. It has gone from slavery to spiritual faith; from spiritual faith to courage; from courage to liberty; from liberty to abundance; from abundance to complacency; from complacency to apathy; from apathy to dependency; and, tragically, from dependency back to slavery."*

Note: America is over 230 years old.

If we examine the history of America and current characteristics of attitude and reaction, it would seem we are entering into the Apathy stage. This is indicated by an increasing tendency on the part of the people to dependency and to withdraw from governmental concerns and assume an attitude that says; "What I do politically doesn't really mean anything anyway." Their reaction is a natural one when faced with a complex, entrenched and expansive bureaucracy governed by unresponsive representatives.

This pattern of degradation may be inevitable. Perhaps it is the nature of people to destroy their societies in this way. History says the odds are against us. But, if this is true, the American society will have an uneasy conscience as it passes through the last stages of Apathy and Dependence. This nation is the first nation in history that was formed with the dangers of excessive government clearly in mind. We are warned by our Constitution, The Bill of Rights and our founding history.

If our founding principles cannot be made to work, if our people cannot make sound readjustments and maintain effective control of their government, <u>then there is no governmental system known to mankind that will not eventually be destroyed by its parental society.</u>

EFFECTS OF OVER-GOVERNMENT

Generally it can be said that those nations with the greatest centralization of government have the least freedom for the individual and furthermore exhibit the worst results in terms of what is desirable in society.

Some governments, such as the Communist type, can excel in certain areas of endeavor by using dictatorial force to generate powerful action. But as far as overall results go, they are complete failures. An especially noteworthy lack in such societies is that of intellectual and creative accomplishments. This lack develops because the pervasive governmental influences existing in such societies smother the will and drive of individuals.

The History of the Soviet Union, the USSR begins with the Russian Revolution of 1917. Communism was implemented across the territories of the former Russian Empire. World War II devastated much of the USSR. One out of every three World War II deaths was a citizen of the Soviet Union. After World War II, the Soviet Union's armies occupied Eastern Europe, where Communist governments came to power in a Soviet bloc.

After many years of the "Cold War", the Soviet Union collapsed in 1991 when Boris Yeltsin seized power. While losing control over many of its satellite nations, Russia has since struggled to establish a market style economy within a democracy. The government still retains strong socialistic tendencies and even shows tendencies to reestablish controls over its satellite nations and a more autocratic government under Putin.

ECONOMIC SYMPTOMS OF EXCESSIVE GOVERNMENT

The government, when it takes over the operation of businesses, short circuits the energy and stimulation and disciplines of free enterprise and free will. The result is a loss of extra individual efforts with the summed results suffering. Adam Smith, an economist of nearly two centuries ago, explained in his book, "The Wealth of Nations":

"It is only for the sake of profit that any man employs a capital in the support of industry; and he will always, therefore, endeavor to employ it in the support of that industry of which the produce is likely to be of the greatest value. He generally, indeed, neither intends it promote the public interest, nor knows how much he is promoting it. By directing that industry in such a

manner as its produce may be of greatest value, he intends only his own gain, and he is in this, as in many other cases, led by an invisible hand to promote an end which has no part of his intention. Nor is it always the worse for society that it has no part in it."

Adam Smith's "invisible hand" functions intuitively through all the individuals and businesses dealing in the free market. This is why it represents the best working process that is capable of perpetually adjusting and improving mankind's economic situation for the good. Governments can never hope to achieve these perfections of control. They can and do upset and restrict these functions by excessive regulations and interference.

SOCIAL EFFECTS OF EXCESSIVE GOVERNMENT

For excessive governmental intensification to take place, it is essential that the people become gradually willing to give up their rights and freedoms and to compromise their principles. A drift toward rule flexibility and away from guiding ideals is part of the pattern of national degradation. It is clearly evident in the histories of fallen nations and, to a large extent, in our own modern, national trends.

The cultural and religious life in our society is especially symptomatic of weakening moral strength. Fundamental religious principles that have given mankind strength through the centuries are diluted with materialistic sophistication till they become meaningless. The beauty and art of the ages is rejected in favor of transient modern experimentation and radical expression. The enduring positive inheritances from the past speak of strength and depth and those who are weak in character and moral courage are made uncomfortable by their examples.

INTERNATIONAL EFFECTS OF EXCESSIVE GOVERNMENT

Usually the intensification of government within a society corresponds directly to a loss of national internal strength and international stature. This pattern is clearly evident in many of the European nations. It can also be said that the United States has sustained definite losses in stature and dignity. These losses have especially been notable during the recent years when the greatest expansions and centralization of government power have taken place.

Our foreign embassies and offices have been abused and damaged and embassy personnel killed. Our word and promises of support have been found to be undependable. We have been forced to withdraw from strategic locations and have allowed the establishment of enemy strongholds in this hemisphere and near our shores.

We have been judged as being economically irresponsible, as is evidenced by general concern over the size of the national debt and the deteriorating value of the dollar. Those who would fund our debts are concerned about these trends and are more and more reluctant to continue lending to meet our needs. ts.

FREEDOM - THE INDIVIDUAL AND GOVERNMENT

About the time our original 13 states adopted their new Constitution, in 1787, Alexander Tyler, a Scottish history professor at the University of Edinburgh, had this to say about the fall of the Athenian Republic some 2,000 years prior:

"A democracy is always temporary in nature; it simply cannot exist as a permanent form of government."

"A democracy will continue to exist up until the time that voters discover that they can vote themselves generous gifts from the public treasury. From that moment on, the majority always votes for the candidates who promise the most benefits from the public treasury, with the result that every democracy will finally collapse due to loose fiscal policy, which is followed by a dictatorship."

"The average age of the worlds greatest ivilizations from the beginning of history, has been about 200 years. During those 200 years, these nations always progressed through the following sequence:

1. From bondage to spiritual faith;

2. From spiritual faith to great courage;

3. From courage to liberty;

4. From liberty to abundance;

5. From abundance to complacency;

6. From complacency to apathy;

7. From apathy to dependence;

8. From dependence back into bondage "

The United States is now in the "complacency to apathy" phase of democracy, with some 45+ percent of the nation's population already having reached the "governmental dependency" phase.

The critical point is when the number of people receiving on government entitlements passes 50% and can control future elections. Today, 45% of US citizens pay no income tax. From that point, the party that promises the most free entitlements wins.

Unfortunately, less than 50% of the population will soon be paying the taxes to support the majority. It will not be long after that the country will be bankrupt. If one considers the current $18+ Trillion National Debt and continuing annual deficits along with all the unfunded liabilities, actual insolvency could be in the near future.

Then, Atlas America will have to shrug its world support and reduce its national services.

One can look at history and see how these patterns of national rise and decline would indicate that citizens living in a democracy will always governmentalize their society to extinction. A feeling of inevitability can be developed. But our forefathers wrote the

Constitution so that, supposedly, we would be able to exercise effective restraints and controls.

FREEDOM AND INCENTIVES

Government destroys incentive and character through the excessive application of taxation, controls and welfare dependency. Note that it is excessive applications that are destructive. Certain appropriate taxation, control and safety net functions are undeniably necessary in any orderly society. But it is in politicians tendency to succumb to the power to excessively expand these functions that the danger exists.

Eric Hoffer, in his book "The Ordeal of Change", drew on his studies of past societies to comment on bureaucratic influences on free trade:

"In a scribe dominated society the trader is regulated off the face of the earth. When the scribe comes into power he derives a rare satisfaction from tearing tangible things out of the hands of practical people and harnessing these people to the task of achieving the impossible and often killing them in the process."

A WELFARE ENVIRONMENT

If an environment develops where welfare becomes a way of life, such as we see in the slums and urban core areas of larger cities, the people in these areas will become semi-permanent wards of the government. They and their children especially, will learn and come to believe that sustenance can be had for nothing.

Those adults in poverty areas who suffer from physical disabilities or who live under handicaps of racial or ethnic discrimination deserve help. Few will disagree that valid needs exist. So, the great and important question is how to create selective, effective aid programs for those who need and deserve help. The keys to success in such programs lie in the personal touch and in the extent of aids given. Welfare actions must be locally designed and carefully administered so as to be truly effective and to minimize their destructive effects.

Massive, poorly administered doles with minimal qualification will create masses of kept citizens who will little resemble free and independent human beings. Politicians who advocate massive federal programs to solve slum problems do not recommend sound solutions, but are seeking to create gigantic power structures in which to shelter their kept constituency.

LAW AND FREEDOM

The individual must be restrained from committing irresponsible, criminal acts that are harmful to other members of the society. Laws and government functions that are created to provide this sort of control generally improve a society's basic character. If the law solely functions to provide protection for individual rights, it will not go wrong. It is only when government takes up the role of resolver of social and economic inequalities that it enters dangerous waters. For then the people must form pressure groups to insist that they receive their shares.

The police and militia, instead of putting their full effort toward fighting crime and keeping peace, will become more and more involved in quelling riots and controlling demonstrations. Thus, law enforcement and social order collapses. The pattern is as old as Rome and Athens and still we make the same mistakes.

CONSTITUTIONAL RESTRAINTS

The Constitution of the United States is unique among the constitutions of the world in the way it was written to restrict the Federal Government from interfering with the rights of individuals. Contrast the way the Russian Constitution is written with the way the American Constitution is written.

Article 125 of the Russian Constitution states:

"In Conformity with the interests of the working people and in order to strengthen the Socialist system, the citizens of the USSR are guaranteed by law: (a) Freedom of speech; (b) Freedom of the press; (c) Freedom of assembly, including the holding of mass meetings; (d) Freedom of street processions and demonstrations."

These civil rights are ensured by placing at the disposal of the working people and their organizations; printing presses, communications facilities, and other material requisites for the exercise of these rights.

In contrast, the United States Constitution states:

"Congress shall make no Law...abridging the freedom of speech, or of the press; or the right of the people peaceably to assemble, and to petition

the government for redress of grievances," and "the right of the people to be secure in their persons, houses, papers and effects shall not be violated and no person shall be deprived of life, liberty or property without due process of law; nor shall private property be taken for public use without just compensation".

Section 8 of the US Constitution defines the authorized powers of the Federal Government:

The Congress shall have power to lay and collect taxes, duties, imposts and excises, to pay the debts and provide for the common defense and general welfare of the United States; but all duties, imposts and excises shall be uniform throughout the United States;

To borrow money on the credit of the United States;

To regulate commerce with foreign nations, and among the several states, and with the Indian tribes;

To establish a uniform rule of naturalization, and uniform laws on the subject of bankruptcies throughout the United States;

To coin money, regulate the value thereof, and of foreign coin, and fix the standard of weights and measures;

To provide for the punishment of counterfeiting the securities and current coin of the United States;

To establish post offices and post roads;

To promote the progress of science and useful arts, by securing for limited times to authors and inventors the exclusive right to their respective writings and discoveries;

To constitute tribunals inferior to the Supreme Court;

To define and punish piracies and felonies committed on the high seas, and offenses against the law of nations;

To declare war, grant letters of marque and reprisal, and make rules concerning captures on land and water;

To raise and support armies, but no appropriation of money to that use shall be for a longer term than two years;

To provide and maintain a navy;

To make rules for the government and regulation of the land and naval forces;

To provide for calling forth the militia to execute the laws of the union, suppress insurrections and repel invasions;

To provide for organizing, arming, and disciplining, the militia, and for governing such part of them as may be employed in the service of the United States, reserving to the states respectively, the appointment of the officers, and the authority of training the militia according to the discipline prescribed by Congress;

To make all laws which shall be necessary and proper for carrying into execution the foregoing powers, and all other powers vested by this Constitution in the government of the United States, or in any department or officer thereof.

Amendments IX and X were added in the BILL of Rights to further clarify the restrictive nature of the Constitution. Amendment IX states:

"The enumeration in the Constitution of certain rights shall not be construed to deny or disparage others retained by the people."

Amendment X states:

"The powers not delegated to the United States by the Constitution, nor prohibited by it to the States, are reserved to the States respectively, or to the people."

The difference would seem to be abundantly clear. Under the Communist/Socialist forms of government, the national government provides the rights for the people. Under the American Constitutional form of government, the Federal Government is restricted from interfering with these rights.

The Constitution of the United States more severely limits the powers and extent of the government than any ever has before. It is this restraint of government, combined with resulting freedom and incentives for the individual that have caused this country to achieve the success it has.

The checks and balances of government defined by the Constitution and the severe limitations placed on the Federal Government are fundamental keys in this matter of control. <u>Our present danger lies in the fact that these restraints and restrictions have been weakened and voided and are being made meaningless.</u>

CHECKS AND BALANCES

Through liberal interpretations of the "General Welfare" and Commerce clauses in the Constitution, the Federal Government has moved in to deal with problems concerning education, public utilities, banking, insurance, business, agriculture, social welfare and a multitude of other areas that find no clear authorization in the Constitution.

Unfortunately, it is clear that the checks and balances are not functioning as intended by the Constitutional authors. The Federal Government is now a massive complex with incomprehensible powers. The expansive forces within this structure in combination with the beneficiaries of its programs and lobbying influences represent explosive potentials for government growth.

Ronald Reagan said, the most frightening words a citizen can hear is *"I'm from the Federal Government and I'm here to help you."*

He also said *"It is not that we are taxed to little, it is that the government spends too much"*.

The cry of a dying society is *"Stop saving me!"*

GROWTH OF THE FEDERAL GOVERNMENT

Growth of Federal Spending and Employment

In 1910 the Federal Budget was 2.6% of total personal income. There were 349,600 Federal employees.

In 2015 the Federal Budget $3.8 Trillion or 16% of USA Gross Domestic Product (GDP). There are 2,100,000 Non Postal, Federal employees. The Federal Debt is $18+ Trillion. This is larger than the Annual USA GDP; ~$16Trillion.

Since 1990, average compensation for Federal workers has increased by 129% as compared to 74% for private sector workers.

Leonard E. Read defined another way that government finances its operations besides taxation, **Inflation**:

"Whenever the take of the people's earned income by government reaches a certain level—20 or 25 percent—it is no longer politically expedient to pay for the costs of government by direct tax levies. Governments then resort to inflation as a means of financing their ventures. By "inflation" I mean increasing the volume of money by the national government's fiscal policy.

Governments resort to inflation with popular support because many people do not realize that they cannot continue to enjoy so-called "benefits" from government without having to pay for them. They do not appreciate the fact that inflation is probably the most unjust and cruelest tax of all.

The U.S. started to gradually move away from the Gold Standard with the adoption of the Bretton Woods system after World War II. With the Bretton Woods Agreement, the world's currencies were pegged to the dollar, which in turn was pegged to Gold at a rate of $35 per ounce.

Under President Nixon the Bretton Woods establishment began to crumble. Pressure took hold on the U.S. to abandon Bretton Woods, so international currencies could be freely valued on the market. The U.S. unilaterally terminated Bretton Woods in 1971, causing the U.S. dollar to effectively become the "reserve currency" for every country.

New dollars are issued when the Federal Reserve elects to fund the purchase of debt, primarily U.S. Treasury Bonds. Essentially printing money.

Dollar Purchasing Power Devaluation

Notice, this chart only goes to the year 2000. How much more has the purchasing power of the dollar been devalued in the last 12 years with the Federal Reserve printing money to stimulate the economy? Today the value of an ounce of gold is $1,000 +.

GROWTH OF THE FEDERAL INCOME TAX

The federal income tax represents a prime example of federal expansionism. Its growth closely parallels the growth of the Federal Government. Income taxation was not a power originally granted to the Federal Government by the Constitution. It was added by the 16th Amendment in 1313. It was initially a modest levy with a normal rate of one percent on personal incomes up to $20,000, a surtax up to a maximum of six percent at $500,000 and a flat corporate tax of one percent. It was said. The sole purpose was to raise revenue. Personal exemptions relieved all but the well-to-do from the tax. When one of the legislators objected and suggested that the tax might some day rise to as high as ten percent, he was shouted down as being unrealistic.

The tax has now risen to 35% percent in the highest bracket. Personal exemptions have been drastically reduced and the corporate rate has been increased to 35%, the 3rd highest in the world. The main burden of the tax is now borne by the upper and middle income groups while the high income groups are given little incentive to provide capital for industry and new enterprises.

Federal Personal Income Tax Paid

Ranked by Adjusted Gross Income

Top 1%   38%

Top 5%   59%

Top 10%   70%

Top 25%   86%

Top 50%   97%

Bottom 50%   3%

The nation is now burdened by many taxes:

Accounts Receivable Tax, Building Permit Tax
CDL license Tax, Cigarette Tax, Corporate
Income Tax, Federal Income Tax, Federal
Unemployment Tax, Food License Tax,Fuel
Permit Tax
Gasoline Tax, Inheritance Tax, Interest expense,

Inventory Tax, IRS Penalties (tax on top of tax), Liquor Tax, Luxury Taxes, Medicare Tax, Property Tax, Real Estate Tax, Social Security TaxState Income Tax, Road usage Taxes, Sales Taxes Recreational Vehicle Tax, School Tax, State Income Tax, Telephone federal excise tax Telephone federal universal service fee tax, Telephone federal, state and local surcharge taxes Telephone minimum usage surcharge tax Telephone recurring and non-recurring charges tax Telephone state and local tax, Telephone usage charge tax, Utility Taxes, Vehicle License, Registration Tax, Vehicle Sales Tax Workers Compensation Tax Etc.

Not one of these taxes existed 100 years ago, and our nation then was the most prosperous in the world. We had no national debt and had the largest middle class in the world.

LOSS OF MONETARY SIGNIFICANCE

Citizens today have lost a sense of monetary significance, especially when hearing politicians explain spending intentions and facts. Their perceptions of the dimensions and amounts of money actually involved with monetary terms such as; Millions, Billions, or Trillions are often meaningless or unrealistic.

Testing your monetary understanding

1. What is the largest US $ denomination bill circulated?

2. How many $100 bills make up $1 Million dollars?

3. A Million Dollars equals how many Thousand Dollars?

4. A Billion Dollars equals how many Thousand Dollars?

5. A Billion Dollars equals how many Million Dollars?

6. A Trillion Dollars equals how many Million Dollars?

7. A Trillion Dollars equals how many Billion Dollars?

The term $1 Billion has lost its significance for most Americans. Most people have no real sense of the reality of one Million dollars let alone Billions or Trillions of dollars. State Government budgets now routinely run into the Billions. Federal budgets and the Federal debt are now

Trillions of Dollars. Government officials casually discuss and authorize the taxing, distribution and spending of Billion and even Trillion dollar sums.

As one government leader once said, *"A $Billion here and a $Billion there, pretty soon you are talking real money!"*

The term "$ Trillion" has become meaningless. Its use obscures the dangerous nature of national spending, budgets and debts.

Not too long ago, a $ Billion ($ One Thousand Million) as the maximum sum used to describe spending. Even true value of $ One Billion is not clearly understood by most people.

$1 Billion = A stack of $1 bills **75 miles high.**

$1 Trillion = One Thousand Billions.

Politicians should not be allowed to state expenditures in Trillions of Dollars.

For instance in 2011, the Annual Federal Budget was $3 Thousand, 600 Billion Dollars ($3.6 Trillion).

The Annual Federal Budget Deficit (borrowed funds) is

$680 Thousand Million ($680 Billion Dollars).

The Federal Debt is $18+ Thousand Billion Dollars ($18+ Trillion).

State budgets now run in the Billions of dollars and Federal budgets in the Trillions of dollars. Federal budget deficits routinely ran into Hundreds of Billions of dollars even Trillions of dollars.

The Power of 1,000

$1 Million = $10,000 $100 dollar bills

$1 Million = $1,000 X 1,000 = $1,000,000

$1 Billion = $1,000,000 X 1,000 = $1,000,000,000

$1 Trillion = $1,000,000,000 X 1000 = $1,000,000,000,000

The Physical Dimensions of Money

$1 Million = A stack of $1 bills **396 Feet high**

$1 Billion = A stack of $1 bills **75 Miles high**

$1 **Trillion** = A stack of $1 bills **75,000 Miles high** or **9.4 times around the world**

$1 BILLION in ½" packages of $10,000 of $100

Bills

1Trillion in ½" packages of $10,000 of $100 bills

The next time you hear politicians speak of Billion and Trillion dollar budgets and expenditures, consider the physical dimensions of the money they are spending for a more realistic perspective.

When a politician says he is proposing to spend $1 Billion for a project, ask him if it is worth 1,000 Million Dollars? See if his answer shows that he clearly understands what a Billion Dollars truly represents.

Test Answers:

1. What is the largest US $ denomination bill circulated? <u>A $100 bill.</u>

2. How many $100 bills make up $1 Million dollars? <u>10,000 $100 bills.</u>

3. A Million Dollars equals how many Thousand Dollars? <u>1,000.</u>

4. A Billion Dollars equals how many Thousand Dollars? <u>1,000,000</u>

5. A Billion Dollars equals how many Million Dollars? 1,000

6. A Trillion Dollars equals how many Million Dollars? <u>1,000,000</u>

7., A Trillion Dollars equals how many Billion Dollars? 1,000

EVALUATIONS AND RE-EVALUATIONS

The great historian of Rome, Theodore Mommsen, when he visited our country more than sixty years ago, was asked what he thought of our country. He replied,

"With more than two thousand years of European experience before your eyes, you have repeated every one of Europe's mistakes. I have no further interest in you."

How many more mistakes have we made during the last sixty years?

Benjamin Franklin was even more pessimistic when he predicted that the Federal Union:

"Can only end in despotism as other forms have done before it when the people shall become so corrupt as to need despotic government, being Incapable of any other."

These are bleak words indeed from these great men, but certainly all who truly love America and understand the principles upon which it was founded must feel a need to strive for a better result. If these principles cannot be made to work, if our people cannot make sound readjustments and maintain effective control of their government, **then there is no governmental system known to mankind that will not eventually be destroyed by its parental society.**

What must be accomplished in our society today is a general, public re-evaluation and re-assessment of the original system of checks and balances, with special consideration being given to why they failed and how they or others which are more effective can be re-established and effectively maintained.

In Article 15 of the Virginia Declaration of Rights, which was drafted by George Mason and adopted in 1776, there appears this statement:

*"No free government or the blessings of liberty can be preserved to any people but by firm adherence to justice, moderation, temperance, frugality, and virtue and by frequent **recurrence to fundamental principles**."* The time for "recurrence to principles" is long overdue.

PART III

CONSERVATIVE PRINCIPLES

Leonard E. Read, President of the "Foundation for Economic Education", defined a basic concept of limited government which well summarizes the role of government in a society according to a conservative viewpoint:

"Government should defend the lives and property of all citizens equally. This means protecting willing exchange and restraining unwilling exchange, suppressing and penalizing fraud, misrepresentation, predatory practices; invoking a common justice under written law; and keeping the records incidental to these functions. Government's legitimate purpose is to codify and then inhibit all destructive actions while leaving all creative and productive actions including welfare, charity, security, and prosperity to citizens acting voluntarily, privately, cooperatively, or competitively, as they freely choose."

THE ROLE OF THE STATES

A major part of Conservatism is the promotion of state supremacy in matters of social/economic functions of government. This is a sound concept, for social, welfare and educational functions are undoubtedly best performed at the state or local levels. To be more explicit, the states have reached tax ceilings. State legislators know that the people are tax saturated. State budgets now run into the Billions of $. They cannot increase taxes to meet the new problems as they arise without encountering powerful opposition. Most states require that their annual budgets must be balanced.

The Federal Government, however, is more flexible financially. Through deficit budgeting, printing money and other fiscal maneuvers, and by virtue of the fact it gets the greatest bite of tax dollars, it can and does respond to these national problems.

It is because of this that we saw the gradual shift to what President Johnson called "Creative Federalism". The shift has gone so far that more than 50 percent of the federal budget is now spent on functions that are not clearly authorized in the Constitution. Many of these are more properly state local functions but the trend continues.

Most people do not have a real sense of how much money and massive power a $3.8+ Trillion Federal Budget represents. Their minds cannot truly comprehend such large numbers. Along with the lobbyists, the special interests and entrenched bureaucracy involved, all this power and money has the potential to overwhelm and corrupt the best intentioned politicians.

Our nation is extremely complex with extensive freedoms of communications, speech and action that allow all expressions of philosophy and sentiment. <u>It must be admitted that today a great portion of government functions at the national level are not authorized in the US Constitution.</u>

Democratic societies seldom change their basic forms of government in drastic, abrupt ways. It has been said that seldom is liberty lost all at once. Adjustments to better, free government should also be made slowly and peacefully. Changes in direction can be accomplished and gradual pursuit of new directions can be successfully implemented. If Libertarian/Conservative philosophies are to gain strength again it will probably be through gradual processes following a redirection of national constitutional policy.

REAGAN CONSERVATISM

The conservative principles that have the greatest acceptance today among moderate and conservative Republicans alike are similar to those advocated by President Reagan. Having started his political career as a New Deal Democrat, after joining the Goldwater candidacy he promoted a new, pragmatic blend of political philosophy seeing excess government as an enemy of American principles along with a positive image of America as "a shining city on a hill". He was a conservative reformist who was fond of Tom Paine's adage, "*We have it in our power to begin the world over again.*"

The fundamental fact about Reagan's conservatism is not just that it is Conservatism but that it is also patriotic and positive. Reaganism has survived and is strongly supported by the Republican Party because it goes with the grain of American culture. It taps into many of the deepest sentiments in American life; freedom, religiosity, capitalism, patriotism, individualism and optimism.

After Reagan, during Bush Presidencies, the Republican Party became more and more accepting of an expanding role for the Federal Government. With the terrorist destruction of the Trade Towers in New York in 2001, a justification for War On Terror expansion of Homeland bureaucracies and Defense spending was created. The Iraq and Afghanistan wars were started leading to more than a decade of loss of life and financial expenditure with little real accomplishment for American interests.

Lack of regulation played a part in bringing about a major recession that began in 2007 and continues in the slowest recovery since the World War II. There were no regulations that stopped the financial and banking institutions from creating the credit swap and elaborate mortgage exchange systems that became the "toxic assets" mess that caused the recession to be so severe.

The "toxic assets'" were the defective mortgages given to unqualified buyers that were encouraged by Federal Government policies implemented through the mortgage management programs "Freddy and Fanny". When these bad mortgages were distributed throughout the financial and banking systems and defaults began, the entire, world, financial systems were affected. Presidents Bush and Obama used unprecedented bail out expenditures to counteract financial impacts and stimulate the economy.

PART IV

REVITALIZATION: A FEDERAL / STATE BALANCE - ESSENTIAL

If an effective alternative is to be developed to oppose the trend to excessive federalism, the role of the states and localities must be revitalized so that they can effectively respond to new problems and so that welfare, social and educational functions can be returned to them. It is hypocritical to hear present day politicians expounding the notion that the problems that arise should be handled by the states and that the states are neglectful in not assuming these duties. The states do not have access to the additional financial resources that would be needed to make them truly responsive. This lack on the part of the states must be recognized as the primary reason that we see an ever expanding federal Government in responding to the social/economic environment of this nation.

Recently, some national leaders have been providing an answer to state tax problems in which the Federal Government makes direct mandates and tax "rebates or grants" to the states. Some mandates are made without supporting grants. This still represents a usurpation of state taxing powers. Federal controls and Influences come with any money so provided. The federal legislators would be remiss in their duties if they did not insist on some controls, if not initially, then gradually. So the federal growth process continues. The people lose by the delays and ineffective applications that must be inherent in such a system. Certainly such money is considerably devalued by federal actions by the time it was returned to the states and put to useful purpose. Clearly, the proper approach is to keep the tax money where it will be used in the first place where and whenever possible.

Decentralization and democracy, these are imperatives in any form of government that would, hope to achieve and retain a healthy balance of freedom and effective governmental responsiveness. Democracy is heavily promoted in our nation which is constitutionally defined as a Republic. Very little, however, is heard about the importance of decentralization though this concept is heavily stressed in our constitution.

Felix Morley stated; *"Indeed one of the great virtues of Federalism is the power given to constituent units* (states) *to adopt experimental measures in accordance with the wishes of local majorities, without imposing such developments on sections not ready or willing to go along. Political democracy is thus localized or qualified but in no sense denied under the American system.*"

NEW CONCEPTS OF GOVERNMENT

What is needed are ways to accomplish a "recurrence to constitutional principles" thereby returning constitutional rights to the people and providing for a government that is constitutional, effective and yet responsive to the nation's needs and restoring liberty to the individual, dignity to the legislature and purpose to the ballot box.

We must seek out, promote and support national leaders who will advocate not only duties of the people but also functional checks and balances for government. These must be leaders who will insist that equality consists not of equal, imposed condition but of an equal right for individuals to compete with others under the American system to achieve their full potential.

These must be those who will insist that government must become, once again, truly constitutional whether this means an update of the constitution or an update of governmental structures, probably both. <u>For, as things exist now, our national government is on a dangerous path of essentially limitless extension and expansion to the point of national debt default.</u>.

The creative imagination and energies of all concerned Americans must be brought to bear on these problems. Ways must be found to define and promote the role of effective, responsive government in a free society. Such government:

1. Must be efficiently responsive to valid functional needs at both the state and federal levels.

2. It must establish and retain efficient functions at the lowest appropriate level of control.

3. It must be self-disciplining with effective oversight, operational checks and balances.

4. It must possess effective processes of periodic function of oversight, review, rejustification and adjustment.

5. Its functions must be Constitutionally authorized, responsible and controlled.

6. It must be fiscally responsible operating within a defined, fully funded budget

EFFECTIVE, RESPONSIVE GOVERNMENT

The inability of the Federal Government to effectively control illegal immigration shows how politics and bureaucracies influenced by pressure groups make effective immigration policies difficult to implement. Democrats are reluctant to really stop illegal immigration because, with amnesty, they see potential Democratic voters.

Republicans do not act on illegal immigration because of the business influence that likes the cheap labor. Border walls proposed are simply token efforts that cannot effectively control thousands of miles of border. Even if built, such lengthy walls will be climbed over or under and breached when patrols are unable to stop them.

The most effective solution to the illegal immigration problem is to eliminate the illegal immigrant job magnet by providing employers the means to accurately identify illegal employees and to penalize businesses that still knowingly hire illegal aliens.

U.S. law requires companies to employ only individuals who may legally work in the United States – either U.S. citizens, or foreign citizens who have the necessary authorization. Enforce this law. **Fine employers who hire non-verifiable, illegal aliens**

E-Verify is an Internet-based system that allows businesses to determine the eligibility of their employees to work in the United States. **E-Verify** is fast, free and easy to use – and it's the best way employers can ensure a legal workforce.

E Verify, Is available to Computer Check for legal immigrant status. **Use** E Verify and **require ,under penalty, legal status** in applications for:

Employment, Health Care, Food Stamps, Education, Welfare, Driver License, etc.

Ensure that only **<u>authorized</u>** citizens or foreigners can get jobs or benefits. Provide temporary work permits for needed immigrant workers. Then;

A border fence will not be needed. No reason to illegally immigrate; no jobs or benefits.

Resident Illegals will be forced to self deport.

By eliminating immigrant job potentials and any support systems that encourage them, they will return to their country and, if interested, will choose to utilize legal immigration processes to come to America and become legitimate citizens.

A government that is truly responsive is one that will react in a prompt, effective manner to new problems that arise. By remaining financially and operationally efficient, it will be capable of such response. To remain efficient implies the existence of continual, viable, active processes of functional oversight, renewal, adjustment and elimination. Efficiency can only come with a high degree of control and intelligent control can only come through a close relationship with the people governed. These are delicate, fragile relationships that can easily be destroyed as has been shown by history.

A concept of effective government represents a philosophy that can be politically successful because it is positive and appeals to mankind's reasoning power. What is truly lacking as an alternative to "greater government" concepts is a reasoned approach to the use of federal powers. Such an approach would give full recognition to the fact that certain federal social / economic functions are necessary. At the same time; it would recognize the fact that whenever such functions are necessary and are established, they represent a great danger and must be subjected to extra special controls and disciplines to ensure that they continue to remain appropriate and necessary functions at the federal level.

LAW IN A FREE SOCTETY

The application of law in welfare, social or educational matters is extremely dangerous as was explained by the French statesman and economist Fredrick Bastiat over 100 years ago to the people of France. At that time in his book "The Law", he told them:

"If you attempt to make the law religious, fraternal, equalizing, philanthropic, industrial, literary or artistic - you will then be lost in an uncharted territory, in vagueness and uncertainty, in a forced utopia or, even worse, in a multitude of utopias, each trying to seize the law and impose it upon you. This is true because fraternity and philanthropy, unlike justice, do not have precise limits. Once started, where will you stop and where will the law stop itself?"

Fredrick Bastiat also recommended a method of judging whether a law is a good law or a bad law. He said:

"See if the law takes from some persons what belongs to them and gives it to other persons to whom it does not belong ... Then abolish this law without delay, for it is not only an evil itself, but also it is a fertile source for further evils because it invites reprisals. If such a law - which may be only an isolated, case - is not abolished

immediately, it will spread, multiply and develop into a system."

The truths in these words are clearly proven by any evaluation of the world's societies today. In America we have used the law in every way he tells us not to. The French people obviously ignored his advice and history proves again and again that people will not restrict their laws in the ways he suggests. His advice is highly idealistic.

So a realistic supporter, instead of strictly advocating Bastiat's idealism, should assume the role of educators who will sensitize the people to the dangers in the use of the law and advocate the creation of disciplines that will ensure that dangerous uses must be subject to critical, effective controls and management.

Thus, their attitudes toward new needed legislation, especially at the state and local levels, can be effective and positive and they can be recognized as being proponents of reason and moderation in government. Without such an image, their philosophies cannot hope to be politically successful. Perhaps they might be described as Conatitutional Independents.

CONSERVATISM

The term "Conservatism" itself has come to have an especially negative connotation during recent years. The general public equates this term with right wing and, too often, with radicalism or obstructive philosophies.

Roget's International Thesaurus lists the following as being synonymous with "Conservative": *"Unprogressive, reactionary, rightist, right winger, die hard, bitter ender, stand patter, uncompromiser, irreconcilable, intransigent, old fogey, stick in the mud, moss back, hard shell, long hair and, old school."*

These are hardly proper words to use to describe positive American philosophies of freedom. Yet the strongest advocates of basic American principles proudly proclaim the fact they are "Conservatives". They glory in this negative term and then wonder why their propositions do not find wide acceptance. Positive terms should be used by all who would advance principles of freedom and sound American government.

The accepted alternative to the term Conservative is Liberal. Synonymous with Liberal is: *progressive, reactionary, open-minded, generous, broad-minded, moderate, free-thinking, tolerant, progressive, protective, etc.*

The term Liberal has lost favor recently. So the term Progressive is now used more commonly to describe what Liberal used to mean; dynamic, advanced, enterprising, reformist, etc. Progressive is equally definitive of a bias to larger government influences.

Essentially, the principles of constitutionality, freedom and balanced government are Independent Constitutional principles. Let us hear not only of libertarian concepts in relationship to civil liberties. Liberty is preserved through an observance of principles relative to all functions of government and all individual rights.

Often the term "Conservative" is attached as a derogatory label by Liberals. Those who would promote a positive conservative view point would be wise to be alert for such labeling tactics and expose them for what they are when encountered. Suggest that such a Conservative view point is really a "Constitutional Independent" view point. Positive terms should be substituted wherever possible in dialogues such as: constructive, effective, responsive, reasoned, moderate, center, effective, American, independent,enterprising, etc.

The obstructive battle to prevent new legislation is one that enjoys little success because usually the current needs that inspired the proposals are real and possess vital strength. So if conservatives focus their energies against such efforts they will attain and deserve the negative image that develops. Battles against legislation which expands existing government can be much more fruitful because such legislation usually does not possess the sound supporting reasoning that initial legislation does. Also, responsive support of necessary new legislation that fills a real need helps develop a positive image that is essential to consistently win elections. Consistent winning of democratic elections is of course, fundamental to the success of any governmental philosophy.

PART V: SOLUTIONS

There is a great deal of conservative literature available which, through critical analysis, defines the error of our ways and describes what societies would be like if the people and the Federal Government were faithful to Constitutional government. Seldom though, do the authors of this literature propose reasonable, specific actions that can be taken. Usually, they end their exhortations with an appeal for an education of the people that, supposedly, will save the society. History tells us how successful these methods have been.

We cannot expect education alone to return the people to Constitutional Principles once they are as far down the road to socialistic over-government and acceptance of dependent services as we are today.

Part of the reason for this inability to reform governmental institutions is that the supporters of "Big Government" are also conducting massive educational campaigns to condition the people for further acceptance of dependent services and securities. It is well known that a strong liberal bias toward bigger government exists in academia as well as the news media. These advocates are well funded. With promises of solutions to problems and more for everyone, they develop highly effective campaigns of persuasion.

Endless studies ingeniously contrive to provide "new sources of revenue" which are derived from the only true source, the tax-payer-consumer. The tax - spend - elect cycle seems infinitely productive of "Greater Government". Libertarian advocates of conservative austerity have had, and always will have, a difficult time being educationally successful in such a political / educational climate.

Today, the best known proponents of Libertarian Politics are Texas Representatives, Rand and Ron Paul. These are some of their recommendations for a more Libertarian Federal Government:

* Veto any unbalanced budget Congress sends to his desk.

* Refuse to further raise the debt ceiling so politicians can no longer spend recklessly.

* Fight to fully audit (and then end) the Federal Reserve System which has enabled the over 95% reduction of what our dollar can buy and continues to create money out of thin air to finance future debt.

* Legalize sound money, so the government is forced to get serious about the dollar's value.

* End the corporate, lobyist stranglehold on the White House.

* Drive down gas prices by allowing offshore drilling, abolishing highway motor fuel taxes, increasing the mileage reimbursement rates, and offering tax credits to individuals and businesses for the use and production of natural gas vehicles.

* Eliminate the income, capital gains, and death taxes to ensure you keep more of your hard-earned money and are able to pass on your legacy to your family without government interference.

* Oppose all unfunded mandates and unnecessary regulations on small businesses and entrepreneurs.

These Libertarian policies were discussed during the previous election and primary debates. They have a growing group of supporters but far less than were needed to seriously impact Democrat or Republican policies.

Libertarian educational processes should continue to be promoted. This must be done because these processes will reach many of the activists in political life. These activists are relatively few in number but they are the effective means of actual political accomplishment.

Libertarian activists, however, must be given reasonable, attractive programs to promote. The primary reason that Libertarians have such limited success is because they only promote freedom from government programs and offer few new alternatives. This constitutes the great lack in our society today; reasonable, salable alternatives to the programs of "Greater Government", a "Constitutional Independent" philosophy.

It is suggested that here is a frontier of thought and creative need that waits unfulfilled. It is the area of the political spectrum between the Conservative / Libertarian right and the Liberal / Progressive left. It is the task of defining the nature and method of government that is effective, self-disciplining and supporting freedom for the individual.

It demands studies and ideas that will discipline over-extensions of government and at the same time free improperly used governmental resources to reduce government or respond effectively to society's valid needs. It requires definitions of techniques of review and re-justification that can be applied to uproot and prevent stagnation, bureaucratic entrenchment and unwarranted duplication and expansion of government programs. It requires concepts that will identify, minimize and dissolve despotic power structures within our society.

Actions and programs must be developed based on historical perspectives not only on transient deficiencies and needs in our nation today. With a historical viewpoint that soundly considers proven, effective concepts and carefully avoids clear errors, techniques can be devised that will allow a continuing **"recurrence to constitutional principle"**.

This is a challenge for Americans today. A problem cannot be resolved until sufficient symptoms exist to define it. Today we have an abundance of symptoms and the errors of our ways can be clearly defined. The demand for action is squarely up to us today.

We must choose elected leaders who will guide us in a response to this challenge. Educators and students should be especially responsive to these creative needs and studies. Columnists, editorialists and all persons in a position to influence public opinion must help. For if we do not act, if we continue to drift and decay under concepts of "Greater Government", history must judge the fault to be our own.

If current trends to bigger government and greater debt continue, default will be likely. Atlas America will be forced to shrug,

THE GENERAL WELFARE CLAUSE

The "General Welfare" clause in the Constitution which has been interpreted to authorize the present federal actions in welfare, social, business and educational matters is in a general statement at the beginning of Section R of the Constitution; Article I, Section R of the Constitution begins:

"The Congress shall have power to levy and collect taxes, duties, imposts and excises, to pay the debts and provide for the common defense and general welfare of the United States; but all duties, imposts and excises shall be uniform throughout the States.

Section F3 continues on for 17 paragraphs to delegate specific powers to Congress;

To borrow money on the credit of the United States. To regulate commerce with foreign nations and among the States and with the Indian tribes. To establish a rule of naturalization and uniform laws on bankruptcies. To coin money, regulate the value thereof and fix the standard of weights and measures. To provide for the punishment of counterfeiting. To establish post offices. To promote science and useful arts by securing exclusive rights to their writing and discoveries. To constitute tribunals inferior to the Supreme court. To punish piracies on the high seas and offences against the laws Of nations. To declare war. To raise and support armies. To provide and maintain a navy. To make rules for land and naval forces. To provide for calling forth the militia. To provide for organizing the militia. To exercise legislation over such district forts, arsenals, and other needful buildings.

Paragraph 18 states; *To make all laws which shall be necessary and proper for carrying into execution the foregoing powers and all other powers vested by this Constitution in the government of the United. States, or in any department or officer thereof.*

It is clearly evident that none of these Constitutional definitions now authorize many of the vast social and economic functions our Federal Government performs today. The prevalent liberal interpretation takes the words "provide for the general welfare" as a blanket, constitutional, authority for the Federal Government to initiate and carry out any function that the Congress may decide on as being for the general welfare of the nation.

The **Commerce Clause** is an enumerated power listed in the United States Constitution.

(Article I, Section 8, Clause 3). *The clause states that the United States Congress shall have power To regulate Commerce with foreign Nations, and among the several States, and with the Indian Tribes.*

This Clause is also used to justify expansive uses of Federal power.

These interpretations are taken in direct contradiction to the abundance of language in the Constitution which restricts the role of the Federal Government in the society, especially in social/economic matters. It implies a disregard for the intent expressed in the Bill of Rights in the Ninth Amendment:

"The enumeration in the Constitution of certain rights shall not be construed to deny or disparage others retained by the people."

and in the Tenth Amendment:

"The powers not delegated to the United States by the Constitution, nor prohibited by it to the States,

are reserved to the States respectively, or to the people".

This disregard for the restrictive clauses in the Constitution has been allowed since the 1930's. It is likely that the people have allowed this interpretation to take effect because they were reacting to the crushing effects of the depression. They sensed a need for more federal power and flexibility and therefore concurred. After some 80 years of experience with this interpretation, however, it is clear that some reevaluation, **"recurrence to constitutional principle"** is required.

The Federal Government has exceeded reasonable restraints and gives every indication of being capable of endlessly growing and accumulating and centralizing power and debt of all kinds. Perhaps becoming **"Too Big To Survive"**.

If the national debt is to be brought under control, limits must be established on federal government expansion.

We see many of the reasonable powers of the states being gradually usurped by the Federal Government. These extensive power assumptions must be brought under a more definitive control, preferably a constitutional control. If the Constitution is to represent any sort of meaningful guide for governing this nation, clarification of the "General Welfare" clause is required.

One way to restrain Federal spending would be to repeal the 16th Amendment that authorizes the Federal income tax. The repeal could probably never be accomplished, but the process of the states going through the process of attempting the repeal would definitely send a clear message to the Federal Government that it must restrain its exorbitant fiscal ways. This would only be a temporary influence on government and in time big spending would likely resume. Something more permanent and more acceptable is needed.

Today, most American citizens seem to generally agree that the Federal Government should be involved in many areas that do not find specific authorization in the Constitution. The "General Welfare" and "Commerce" clauses can be, and in fact has been, liberally construed to authorize federal activities in almost any field. This has been established in precedent activity and by consensus approval at the polls. Indeed, reasonable thought must find logic in the concept that a national constitution cannot specifically define all the powers of a Federal Government.

Still, dangerous centralization of governmental power can take place and, in fact, has already taken place.

What is needed is an authorization that would, allow the Federal Government to move in where national problems exist but one which would preserve a practical amount of oversight and control as well as decentralization through retention of adequate state and local governmental powers.

One way in which this could be accomplished would be through an amendment to the Constitution which would allow the states to establish a maximum limit on total federal expenditures/budgets.

AN EXAMPLE AMENDMENT

An example draft of a constitutional amendment would help to demonstrate some techniques that would establish some of the governmental disciplines that have been previously discussed and stimulate further considerations that might lead to ideal solutions.

An amendment is here proposed to rectify the dangerous course of our national government and reestablish Constitutional significance. Granted, this amendment would represent a major change in the role of the States relative to the Federal Government. Such strengthening of state influences would be needed if the Federal Government continues to demonstrate continuing inability to effectively manage the nation's fiscal responsibilities.

A FEDERAL LIMIT AMENDMENT

The total annual expenditures of the Federal Government of the United States shall not exceed a limit established at the time of ratification of this amendment except as may be authorized at any time for periods of up to twelve months by at least fifty one percent of the State Legislatures. After ratification of this amendment, all income of the Federal Government of the United States in excess of the established expenditure limit shall be disbursed to the States on the basis of population or shall be used to reduce the national debt.

The states, in original agreement, designed, created and ratified the Constitution of the United States. Ultimately the states must concur in the validity of the US Constitution. If the Federal Government significantly deviates from the specifications in the Constitution, Article 5 defines the right of states to propose and ratify amendments as needed.

Amendment ratification by ¾ of the several States or by conventions.

Ratification of a Federal Limit Amendment would require approval of three fourths of the State Legislatures. **The states would be in favor of such an amendment because of the greater influence they would obtain over growth of the Federal Government and the potential of getting surplus funds.** State's rights and constitutional federalism would be reinforced. This fact would provide a strong incentive for states to use their founding powers and constitutional right to institute a Federal Limit Amendment.

The 26th amendment (granting the right to vote for 18 year-olds) took only 3 months & 8 days to be ratified! Why?   The people demanded it. That was in 1971   before computers, e-mail, cell phones, etc. Of the 27 amendments to the Constitution, seven (7) took 1 year or less to become the law of the land all because of public pressure.

Ratification can also be accomplished through a Constitutional Convention that can be called by two thirds of both houses of Congress or two thirds of the State Legislatures. To make an almost painless transition, the federal limit could be set at the amount of the Federal Budget as of the time of ratification. Thus, its approval would represent no abrupt national upheaval but would constitute a definite act of re-direction that would immediately go into effect.

Basic effects: Basic disciplines would be created by such an amendment;

1. Control of the size and growth of the Federal Government through constitutional budgetary restraints.

2. Debt reduction or dispersion of excess federal funds in a manner that is nationally equitable and not subject to federal political influence.

3. Federal competition for available funds within the limit will increase program oversight, rejustification and the reduction and elimination of unnecessary functions.

4. State competition for available funds would add an additional check and balance effect to the Federal Government.

5. The Constitutional Congressional requirement to declare war would be reinforced. The Vietnam, Iraq and Afghanistan wars would likely not have been authorized and funded with this amendment in effect.

6. States rights and constitutional federalism would be strengthened. This fact would provide a strong incentive for states to use their constitutional right to institute a Federal Limit Amendment.

TOTAL EXPENDITURES CONTROLLED

Note that the total expenditures of the Federal Government would be limited. This would have to include all its functions; defense as well as non-defense spending including what are called discretionary and non-discretionary expenditures. All Federal disbursements must be covered by this limit to ensure that no unauthorized growth can develop. No off budget authorizations can be allowed. The primary reason for such an amendment would be to reestablish a Constitutional Federal Government.

To be effective, such fiscal control must be complete.

While totality of control would have to be affected, it would not be an inflexible control. A simple majority of the State Legislatures could authorize a change in the federal expenditures limit at any time. Such a change would remain in effect for up to twelve months. It is conceivable that a limit expansion would come to be annually re-authorized and carried along year after year. This could occur when a popular expansionist consensus develops and is sustained in a majority of the states. An annual review and renewal on the part of the states would be required but this would certainly be a limit authorization exercise that would ensure a continuing proper role for the Federal Government in relation to the states in the nation.

Serious threats that can be clearly defined such as imminent war or national disaster would certainly stimulate a prompt response for a limit change from a majority of the states if needed. Such clear dangers would easily retain the necessary support and annual limit re-approval. The national administration would have to clearly present the case and move the states to action when dangers threaten national security that will demand resources beyond the budget limit. Indefinite, unclear declarations of national danger would probably find difficulty in getting support in the national budget. Sustaining support for such pseudo threats would he almost impossible to sustain for any significant period of time.

The Constitution was originally authorized by the states of the union. It is the founding power and ratification by the States of America that ultimately give the Federal Government its powers through the Constitution. When it exceeds these powers beyond reason, the states have the constitutional right and duty though amendment to correct any such abuses. This Federal Limit Amendment sets up a subtle but powerful competition for government revenues between the states and within the Federal Government that is flexible in execution and free from inappropriate political influences.

BUDGETARY DISCIPLINES

The concept of using budgetary disciplines and processes to establish fiscal control and administrative management within the Federal Government gave birth to Bureau of the Budget through the Budget and Accounting Act of 1921. The bureau this act created prepares an integrated plan of financial estimates and has specific authority to make studies of the organizations and operations of the executive branch.

The Director and Deputy Director of the Budget are appointed by the President without Senate confirmation. The Budget and Accounting Act of 1921 also laid the legal Framework for unified control over departmental accounts and for a government wide audit system and budget formation in these areas:

The military, commerce and finance, labor and welfare, and resources and civil works legislative reference, management and organization of the executive branch, statistical standard definition and implementation and financial management procedures for all bureaus and departments.

The federal budget process begins at the spring of each year. Overall budgetary policy is defined at the cabinet level. These policies are then disseminated with guidelines and a call for estimates and definitions of intended agency programs. This call is over 12 months in advance of the relevant fiscal year that begins July 1st.

Within each agency, the budget officers obtain estimates from the bureaus and divisions. These estimates are extensively reviewed and examined within the agencies before being submitted to the Budget Bureau examiners. Hearings are then held for the individual Agencies to allow them to defend and clarify proposals and budget requirements. From these hearings and examinations, recommendations are drafted and submitted for approval to the Budget Director and his review groups. After approval by the Director has been obtained, the estimates and highlights of each agency's requirements are submitted to the President for his approval.

At the beginning of the legislative session which begins in January, the President presents the budget prepared by this process in a budget message and by reports to the Congress and the nation. Committees of the Congress review this "Presidential Budget" and Congress, provides guidance in the preparation of appropriation proposals. When these proposals are passed by the Congress, they represent the "Appropriations Act" for that year. The Bureau of the Budget then becomes involved in enforcing the budgetary disciplines imposed by the "Appropriations Act" through out the federal agencies.

It is an indication of how the Federal Government has lost effective control of its fiscal condition in that the Senate failed to pass a budget for over 3 years.

An extensive apparatus exists for governmental cost estimation, review, justification, fiscal procedure and functional audit in the federal budget system. If this system has failed to act as a viable controlling force in government, and federal growth patterns in recent decades would indicate that this is true, it is probably because the Bureau of the Budget is not an unbiased part of the federal power structure. Its purpose is to provide financial analysis of pending legislation and existing services. Indeed, reason would say that, by its nature and function in the federal legislative system, the bureau's biases would have supported the excessive growth patterns.

The Budget Bureau's expertise, methods and system could probably be more effective in a federal environment where, because of constitutionally defined fiscal limits, agencies must compete for available funds. Its audit and accounting systems could be a great aid in locating departments and functions which are weak and not supportable among prevailing priorities. The bureau's broad authorities and review procedures could be a powerful catalyst in the process of governmental discipline and rejuvenation. It could be the communicative and examining force that would help make agency and departmental competition work. Given the incentive of a constitutionally enforced spending limit, the budget system could be more effective in the performance of these vital disciplinary services. For instance, here is an excerpt from the 2012 Annual GAO Report...

The Federal Government Accountability Office GAO annual report addresses duplication and areas for costs savings throughout the federal government; The 2013 GAO duplication report reviewed 51 areas of government spending, including 32 areas of extensive federal duplication, fragmentation and overlap, and 19 areas for large cost savings through addressing waste and mismanagement.

And like last year's report, identified more than $100 billion in budgetary savings by simply eliminating duplicate programs. These findings are a testament to failed congressional efforts of oversight and a reminder that Congress continue to shirk its duty to address even blatant areas of waste and mismanagement of taxpayer funding. Duplication exists throughout every federal agency and every corner of the budget, from the Department of Defense, to special interest tax credits, and every federal agency and office on Constitution Avenue.

The problem in Congress today is not an issue of ignorance. It is one of indifference and incompetence. The scope of the Federal

Government has become too big to be effectively governable.

LIMIT ADEQUACY

How large should the federal sector of government be in our society? There is almost certainly no fixable limit that is proper for all time. Probably as of today, it is too large. Far too many of the present federal functions should be state functions or should be eliminated, reduced or replaced with different, better programs of action at the state and local levels.

It is conceivable that with the passage of an amendment such as the Federal Limit Amendment, the role of the government could be effectively reduced. On the other hand, perhaps not. Perhaps the role of the Federal Government would have to be increased even beyond its present size when the society continues to grow and require more national services. The important thing is that either growth or contraction can occur under constitutional control and a mechanism would exist with a Federal Limit Amendment by which effective control of these processes could be maintained.

USE OF EXCESS FEDERAL FUNDS

A key effect such a limit amendment would have would be to create a reflective ceiling for federal funds. It would be reflective in that it would force dispersion of excess funds collected downward to lower levels of government based on population. Thus, states and, through the states, local governmental units would receive funds free of requirements to enable them to be responsive to the problems and needs of the people or provide tax refunds.

If the federal expenditures ceiling were fixed at the level as of the time of amendment ratification, no immediate funds would be available for dispersion. But with continuing growth in the nation's economy and with income tax rates continuing at the same level, the federal income from taxes would exceed the expenditures limit. This excess income would then become funds dispersable to the states. The Federal Limit Amendment would require that these excess funds be utilized either by allocation to the states on the basis of population or for reduction of the national debt. The Federal Government's only discretionary power regarding such funds would be to decide whether the funds should be given to the states or used to reduce the Federal debt. Of course, the Federal Government would still retain the power to raise or lower taxes as a means of controlling economic cash flow increase or reduction to counteract major inflationary or recessionary trends.

Because the powers of the Federal Government would be limited in this respect, funds allocated to the states could be funds free of federal controls. Thus, effective decentralization of government could be accomplished. On the other hand, the Federal Government would have a strong reason for using the funds to control the national debt effectively. Since the funds could not be used to expand federal powers, the government could be relatively unbiased in its use of such excess funds.

A powerful, safe tool would be provided to deal with problems of the national economy. In times of recession, the Federal Government could choose to disperse excess income downward to the states thereby stimulating the economy. It may even choose to augment these funds with borrowed funds to create greater impacts.

It is important to note that, through the states and local governments the spending would be decentralized and thus more effectively done than would be possible through Washington. In times of inflation, the government could choose to levy taxes to dampen inflationary pressures. In this case, the income from such taxes would be used to reduce the national debt. It could not be used to increase federal functions. In either case, federal growth would be appropriately restricted.

A REASONABLE STEP

Most importantly, ratification of such a Federal Limit Amendment would represent a step toward control establishment that would not demand a drastic deviation from existing governmental policies and governmental functions. It is possible that the limit established at the time of the Constitutional Convention could be set equal to the amount of the prevailing total national budget. Thus, only further federal expansion would be limited and the amendment's effects on society in general would be minimized.

While the turning point affected by such an amendment would not represent an extremely radical departure from national policy, the broad effort involved in creating and ratifying a Federal Limit Amendment would accomplish a powerful rejuvenation of constitutional principles and philosophy within the society. This would represent the psychological aspect of **recurrence to principle** and if these sentiments were properly nurtured and nationally stimulated, they could lead to much wiser and more effective democratic, constitutional processes. The process of constitutional amendment itself would create a valuable refocus on the need for effective, constitutional control.

This may stimulate and strengthen the proposal of other creative disciplines to create effective government controls such as:

 Pay Go policies that require that every new, proposed expenditure must be funded from new taxes or funds from other parts of the budget.

The Presidential Line Veto that would allow the President to eliminate line item spending from bills.

Term Limits for Representatives would also improve government control attitudes by removing incentives for career politicians.

Add **Sunset Provisions** to existing and all new laws to force periodic review and rejustification of need. This would strengthen congressional oversight and recurrence to principle.

Pass a law that requires that any member of congress voting for a budget in which there is a deficit of more than 3% of GDP (Gross Domestic Product) will be ineligible for re-election.

Proposed Amendment to the United States Constitution: "Congress shall make no law that applies to the citizens of the United States that does not apply equally to the Senators and/or Representatives; and, Congress shall make no law that applies to the Senators and/or Representatives that does not apply equally to the citizens of the United States."

The Mack Penny Plan would balance the Federal Budget in8 years by cutting one penny out of every federal dollar spent for 6 years and cap spending at 18% of Gross Domestic Product beginning in the 7th year. If congress fails to make the necessary cuts, the plan triggers automatic across-the-board cut to meet the yearly caps.

With a redirection initiated and emphasis being placed on better principles, national leaders would be chosen and would rise to be caretakers of these principles. Such leaders would then guide the people in developing a society that is controlled by a national government that is truly effective, responsive and yet supportive of freedom in the nation. The current low opinion of the members of Congress would certainly improve with these new results and influences.

It may be that current trends to bigger government with more benefits leading to greater and greater national debt will continue given the inability of Congress to make the tough decisions. **This will eventually cause Atlas America to shrug and insolvency will occur**. It is in that aftermath, major recurrence to effective principles will have to be done. This may be what it takes to finally, seriously consider some of these suggested initiatives.

PART VI

RESULTS AND EFFECTS

Any examination of possible results and effects that might come from the enactment of an amendment such as the proposed Federal Limit Amendment would have. What might happen and what effects could be created. Direct and implicit disciplines would be created by such a limit amendment.

The direct disciplines are those that are explicit in the wording of the amendment. They define the creation and control of the federal expenditure limit and the disposition of any excess funds that might be accumulated. These are very direct disciplines and would probably be effective during the initial years after amendment enactment when the sense and intent of the amendment remains clear in the minds of the people.

Almost certainly, however, elements of the Federal Government would ultimately devise schemes for bypassing or nullifying these disciplines just as they have bypassed the checks and balance systems inherent in our original Constitution. Most likely some of the first efforts would be to develop elements of federal spending that are not reported within the controlled budget.

When such deviations occur, and certainly they would, the task of "**recurrence to constitutional principle**" would fall again to the citizens and their Representatives. Such guards must be a continuing concern if principles that provide freedom from burdensome government are to prevail.

The passage of a Federal Limit Amendment would also create some new implicit disciplines. Those may well be more important than the direct disciplines in that they would force a change in attitudes within government. With a limit on funds available for federal spending, the administrators would have to take a new look at their methods of obtaining funds. Infinitely expandable tax revenues from economic growth or borrowed funds would no longer be available for their disposition.

Assuming the existence of a limit on federal expenditures, proposals for new governmental functions would have to be carefully examined and justified. Their worth would have to be clearly proven. Such worth would have to be carefully weighed within the priorities of all expenditures. To get funds for these new activities, less worthy governmental functions would have to be reduced or made more efficient and effective. The only source of additional funds would be from other parts of the federal budget. A system of competition among agencies and departments would be created. Federal "pork barrel" or "earmark" projects for certain states would be difficult to develop and harder still to maintain through periods of reevaluation.

Functions that are not clearly justifiable would be put under fire and be made truly valuable or eliminated. Review, justification and periodic re-justification would become functional necessities. A primary question to be asked concerning any new proposals or in reviewing existent functions would be; "Is this function really needed and would this function be better performed at a state or local level?"

Duplication of functions in different agencies would have to be to be reviewed and justified and then eliminated or adjusted.

Functions that are truly federal in nature and truly needed would easily make their cases of justification. If the limit were retained at a given level over a period of years, the addition of new needed federal services would force a return of many of the current functions to the states or be eliminated as they should be. Thus, a proper decentralization of control would be accomplished.

The states would play an important role in influencing decisions on federal functions. Significant financial leverages would be available to the states to obtain and retain control of proper state and local functions. Financing could he made available for valid state and local services either by way of return of limit surpluses or by limit adjustment. Even if these leverages were not exercised, their existence would create vital psychological disciplines on the federal system.

On the other hand, the Federal Government would not be rigidly excluded from operating in areas that could be state or local functions. The liberal interpretation of the "General Welfare" clause would still be in effect. This would enable the Federal Government to guide and influence state and local activities in ways that would truly promote the General Welfare of the Nation.

When problems develop in a number of the states in such a way that they apparently represent or threaten to become a national problem, the Federal Government could exercise its "general welfare" powers. It would be especially prone to use such powers if the states appear to be generally insensitive to the problems. Such problems would be debated in a national forum that would attract wide attention. The states would sense that the Federal Government is considering moving into these areas and this knowledge would energize local and state concern regarding the issues. Then, depending on reactions on both levels, actions would develop that would be influenced by competitive concern. The interaction of federal and state biases would force clear distinctions of proper levels of authority for problem solutions. Not only would effective checks exist, balances and action stimulators would be in operation.

PART VII

PROBLEM EXAMPLES AND POSSIBLE EFFECTS

To gain more insight into the possible effects that a disciplinary Constitutional technique such a Federal Limit Amendment might have, some example problems and related functions of the Federal Government will be considered.

The following subjects will be considered; National Economics (National Debt, "New Economics") Problems of the Cities (Welfare and Urban Redevelopment), Civil Rights, War and a Federal Limit.

NATIONAL ECONOMICS

Fiscal responsibility and the economic health of the nation must be a prime concern of governmental leaders as well as citizens. If fiscal irresponsibility adversely affects national economic well being, then not only is the society in danger of ultimate bad effects but, more immediately, financial resources for dealing with current services and problems can be seriously threatened.

It is in the area of national economics that the expansive, accumulative nature of the Federal Government has been most evident in recent years. Budget deficits are almost habitual and, in more recent years, deficits of hundreds of Billions of dollars are not enough. Often, budgets were not even defined. Trillion dollar deficit authorizations were repeatedly made.

The Federal Debt as of January 2007 was over $8.5 Trillion.

The Federal Debt limit was increased to $9 Trillion in 2008.

The bailouts and stimulus programs of 2008 and 2009 are purely deficit spending. The Federal Debt in April 2009 was $12 Trillion. The limit has again been expanded to $18+ Trillion to accommodate additional expenditures.

The estimated population of the United States is 300,600,000.

Each citizen's share of this debt is over $52,000.

Since the fiscal year began on 1 October 2005, debt has grown $2.03 Billion per day.

The debt limit has again been expanded to $18+ Trillions to accommodate the enormous deficits created by the Bush and Obama administrations to counteract the 2008 – 2009 recession.

Regardless of major party affiliation, the national leadership attempts to project an image of concern over federal costs. Each makes token gestures and efforts toward federal fiscal responsibility. But the net effects are clearly evidenced in actual budgetary growth patterns. No plans are even proposed that will actually eliminate the Deficits or reduce the National Debt. Minimal proposals are made that only slow the rate of growth of the Federal Government. Actual cuts are left for future politicians to make.

The 2015 Debt is $18+ Trillion.

By 2020 the debt will likely be over $20 Trillion.

Clearly, legislated Federal spending limits are ineffective. **A specific Constitutional Limit is needed to create a discipline that actually accomplishes real limit control.**

"NEW" ECONOMIC THEORIES

The Keynesian economic theories that gained general academic acceptance and have been implemented since President Kennedy tell us that the Federal Government should "fine tune" the nation's economy along a path of sound growth in line with productivity. As theory, the "New Economics" seems to make sense and it would seem that it could work if used properly. Unfortunately, the Federal Government shows no inclination to properly use such theories.

The necessities of politics and temptations of political power warp and twist and turn the "New Economics" from seemingly sensible economic theory into a monstrous government generator.

Instead we see: *Surpluses* - Quickly absorbed by new functions requiring more government employees, facilities, equipment, etc.

Tax increases - Great reluctance to pass needed tax increases during election years. Devious, gradual taxation increases are accomplished by manipulation of a multitude of tax, fee and tariff sources.

Tax Decreases - Tax decreases are only voted in conjunction with budget deficits to ensure no reduction in governmental income and functions.

National Debt Increases - Habitual and done in greater increments that are totally unjustifiable in an inflationary economy.

Historically, effective control of the scope of government has been an impossible accomplishment in democratic societies. All history seems to say that democracies are only satisfactory as temporary forms of government and that they are incapable of sound perpetuation. This nation's founders recognized this fact and developed a system of government with checks and balances that would properly control the role of government in the society. But now, these founding dreams and principles seem to be inadequate. The checks have been slipped and the balances are askew. **A recurrence to principle is required.**

With a Federal Budget Limit in effect, different attitudes toward national economics would have to develop. First, dangerous federal expansionary trends would be checked. The limit would force research into existing operations to provide the financial resources for any new needed functions. Interdepartmental competition would force a much needed house cleaning. Duplication and unneeded inefficient departments and functions would be eliminated. Functions that would be better done at state or local levels would be removed from the Federal Government. The elimination of unrestricted opportunity for power assumption and expansion would instill a much more reasoned and moral approach to all phases of government. This would be especially important in the area of national economics.

With the disciplinary influence of an expansion limit functioning, congress could make decisions regarding national economic problems from a position that would not be significantly influenced by biases of federal power expansion. Flagrant attitudes of extravagance could not exist because the finances simply would not be there to support them.

There would be much less danger of inflationary trends developing due to irresponsible national fiscal policies. However, should inflationary situations develop that generate surpluses in federal income beyond the limit, the government would not be able to spend these surpluses. This would eliminate a most significant source of fuel feedback for the economic fires. The Federal Government would not be inclined to do deficit spending during inflationary times for it could not expand its own economic, government (power) base.

It might elect to retire the national debt with such surpluses and may well be inclined to do so as an anti-inflationary measure. If inflation were so rampant as to require tax increases, the revenues from such income increases again could be used against the National Debt to stem inflation. A secondary benefit of this is reduction in interest payments on such debts. Tax income could not be used by the government to create new federal functions whose spending would invalidate inflationary dampening as has been the case in the past.

Should recessionary trends set in, the Federal Government could decide to feed federal funds to the states to stimulate economic activity. Such funds would be borrowed by the issuance of federal bonds and notes in the same way that deficit budget expenditures are now financed. Spending such funds through the states would be in line with proper decentralization of functions thereby getting the greatest effectiveness from these funds.

Another method that might be used would be to give a federal tax reduction and make up the difference in the federal income by borrowing procedures. The Important consideration in such economic actions should be that they could be taken for sound economic reasons that would be much less biased from the standpoint of expansion or contraction of the federal power base.

At this point in time, the "New Economics" cannot be said to be proven to be sound and viable principles. The practice of these theories has been badly distorted by political influences and tendencies to federal expansion. The necessities of politics and temptations of political power warp and twist and turn the "New Economics" from seemingly sensible economic theory into a monstrous government generator.

The explicit and implicit disciplines of a "Federal Limit Amendment" would certainly create a better economic and political environment for further testing of the concepts of the "New Economics"

URBAN PROBLEMS

While functioning under a Federal Limit Amendment, how would the government respond to the problems of the cities? Certainly there are problems that require action and solutions. They are widely discussed. They are real and clearly apparent. Air and water pollution, congestion, core city decay, obsolescence or transportation and education systems not to mention a host of serious, special problems that are unique to given areas or localities. The funds required to solve these problems run into the hundreds of Billions of dollars and will represent a continual drain on the economy for the foreseeable future.

The Federal Government is deeply involved and is spending Billions annually to attack these problems. The Department Of Health Education and Welfare which was created by Congressional enactment in 1953 has grown to become a major department with a budget running into the tens of Billions of dollars.

The problems of the cities are immense in scale and infinitely varied in complexity and nature. The solutions required must be similarly varied and accordingly scaled and tailored to fit local situations. If they are to be effective solutions that truly satisfy the problems and people involved, they will probably not; come out of any mold fashioned in Washington. These problems are different in all cities just as all cities are different. The natures of cities and their problems are as unique as their individual geographies, their terms of existence, and the ethnic and cultural backgrounds of their people.

Detroit has recently declared bankruptcy. It has terrible economic and cultural problems. Senator Rand Paul proposes a wide-ranging plan to revitalize the nation's cities through the creation of "economic freedom zones." His plan would cut federal taxes in communities that have an unemployment rate of 12% or more.

Federal personal and corporate taxes would be lowered to 5%, and the federal payroll tax would be cut to 2% each for employees and employers.

"Inside these zones, l suspend the capital gains tax and allow small businesses to deduct most of what they invest," he said.

The plan would save Detroit $1.3 billion over the next 10 years, Paul said.

This is an example of the type of new, innovative thinking that is required to deal with the complex problems in cities. Detroit is not the only city with serious fiscal problems. There are many others. The Federal Government is clearly incapable of providing effective solutions to these problems.

Often the solutions to city problems require the exercise of rights of eminent domain where government forcefully takes ownership of a private property to make a more public beneficial use of it. People must be uprooted and moved. Such work is always delicate and requires a high degree of precise skill and concern to minimize the painful, costly human effects and to ensure that just actions are taken. This is no work for the "Federal Bulldozer". The decisions as to need, initiation, method, extent and timing clearly belong at the local and state levels. The vast costs associated with solutions for the problems of the cities dictate that efficiency in accomplishment is imperative. Extensive decision hierarchies and paper mills cannot be tolerated. The enormous sums of money required should not be routed through Washington for bureaucratic depletion, delay and misdirection.

With a Federal Limit Amendment in effect, state governments would receive federal revenues above the budget limit figure in addition to normal Federal funds. Such excess funds would be dispensed at the state level on a per-capita basis which is not only equitable but suitable to the populous nature of the problems. Such dispensations, free of Washington's discounts and interferences, could be applied in a decentralized manner according to real area and local needs.

Given continued growth in the GDP (Gross National Product) and a Fixed Federal Limit, increasing revenue excesses should prove adequate to meet the problems of population growth and to accomplish the adjustments and renovations needed to save and maintain our cities.

CIVIL RIGHTS

Creation of racial fraternity through the use of government administered economics and legal force is indeed a dangerous experiment. The relatively limited experience we have had with the Federal Government attempting to legislate interracial harmony has clearly demonstrated the truth in Fredrick Bastiat's warning;

"If you attempt to make the law fraternal, equalizing, you will then be lost in an uncharted territory, in vagueness and uncertainty, in a Forced utopia. This is true because fraternity and philanthropy, unlike justice, do not have precise limits. Once started, where will you stop and where will the law stop itself?"

Not only are we beginning to see the "uncharted Federal utopias" but dangerous evidences of interracial and inter-class warfare develop.

Still, there is undeniable truth in the charges of discrimination and bigotry leveled during the years of strife over civil rights. The minority races have been unjustly dealt with and such treatment must be condemned. Clearly there is a role for government in dealing with intolerance and injustice to minorities. Experience would indicate, however, that the role should be one of moral and ethical leadership rather than force in creation of fraternity among citizens. Plenty of laws and rulings have already been made to protect civil rights.

Bigotry and intolerance are ingrained and emotional characteristics that suppressive legal force is more likely to inflame rather than subdue. If these evil human faults are to be ultimately eliminated, it must be done through leadership in example and by ethical persuasion. Most importantly, the persecuted minorities must prove by their actions and lives that the biases are unjustified and unconscionable.

Time and the good influences of leadership and inspiring example are the only possible ultimate remedies for the inequities. While it is difficult for the persecuted minorities to accept this, it is the only way. The alternatives of dependency programs, use of force and legal bribery have led and will continue to lead to damaging actions that will ultimately hurt the afflicted minorities the most. The "War On Poverty" has created a dependent class and created fatherless, disfunctional families. Such solutions prove to be infinitely worse than the problems.

By making funds more available and more effective at local levels, the problems of housing for ghetto dwellers will be better handled. Instead of creating vast jungles of Federal housing projects, a closer relationship to the people can be developed. Through more intimate contacts and flexibility that can adapt to local human needs, solutions that work may be attainable.

A Federal Limit Amendment would probably affect a gradual shift of present federal welfare and educational functions back to the states. Since these are basically and properly state and local functions, the states would likely move to control the federal limit so as to force these functions back to the states. Thus the basic elements of force would be removed from the Federal Government in these matters. However, this would not restrict the role of federal leadership in civil rights. A national forum would still exist to advocate resolution of inequalities.

Where severe conditions of injustice exist so as to arouse the national conscience, special functions of economic and legal force could be created and utilized. Once such functions have served their purpose, they would be eliminated to provide the funds to satisfy other national needs and affected state or states then would proceed in a more enlightened manner.

WAR AND A FEDERAL LIMIT AMENDMENT

The Military Industrial Complex

Where in the world are the 2,500,000 active front-line and reserve military personnel? In 700 bases in 144 nations around the world. Consider the industry, logistics, facilities and equipment costs to support the Military Complex. The proposed 2015 Federal Military Budget is $610 Billion.

President Eisenhower, at the end of his term, warned us of the dangers inherent in the power and influence or what he called a *"military industrial complex"* in our society. Collusion between government and war industry is not new but it must be carefully controlled in a free society. A proper limit to defense and national security expenditures is essential.

In Section 8 of the US Constitution which defines the fiscal powers of the Federal Government, its power to fund the Military is described:

To raise and support armies, but no appropriation of money to that use shall be for a longer term than two years.

In fact no budget of any kind was passed by the Senate for three years.

With a federal budget limit In effect, this nation would be a great deal more careful and justified in entering into international conflict than it has been. Clear reasons would have to develop and be explicitly enunciated by federal leaders to arouse a definite national purpose and thereby cause the states to expand the federal limit. With a federal limit in effect, great pressures would always exist within the national government to utilize all Defense Department and available federal funds. With this situation existing, only wars of absolute necessity and clearest justification would be authorized and fought. Wars would have to be justified with a clear enemy or national threat and defined with clear goals and exit strategies.

The limit amendment would require a simple majority of state legislatures to support necessary limit expansions. This support would have to be renewed annually to provide continuing funds.

Thus, two new checks are created on national war making potential. Specific control of the defense system, the responsibility for national security and the initiative of defining the necessity of war would still reside with the national government.

Where a war is justified, obtaining initial approval by the states would not be difficult and, for as long as the war should be fought, support would be forthcoming. When such a war is finished though, an especially important aspect of the limit amendment would take effect. With the need for war removed, the limit could revert to prewar status at which time the Congress could vote the released funds for deficit reduction, a tax reduction or release the funds for dispersion to the states. Too often in the past, war's end has meant that funds needed for defense during war are used to expand the role of the Federal Government in the society.

The Second World War was a prime example of this process. From 1940 to 1950 the federal budget more than tripled in size. The premise that a tax cut can also stimulate a postwar economy is not given strong consideration at such times. The idea that defense spending must be re-channeled into an expansion of peaceful governmental functions always has prevailed.

A federal limit would eliminate the "greater government" biases at those critical times thereby fostering a much healthier post war adjustment environment.

It is doubtful that the Vietnam, Iraq and Afghanistan wars would have been started or long supported with this type of amendment in effect. Surely the Iraq war would never have been authorized or supported especially as the sectarian violence escalated after Sadam's fall. Support for the war in Afghanistan would be doubtful given the historic failures by Britain and Russia to succeed there. Using the military for Nation Building would be very difficult to support and sustain.

The massive government expenditures and controls authorized by the "War On Terror" would never have gone to the extremes allowed with a limit amendment in effect. The term "War On Terror" is a good example of the technique of over exaggeration of a threat to justify enormous government expansion. A "War On Terror" will likely never see a definable end. Terror is a reaction and terrorism is a tactic not a nation state to be attacked. One cannot wage war on a reaction or tactic to any satisfactory conclusion.

Terrorism has been practiced throughout history and will be with us in the future in one form or another. Wars fought in Iraq and Afghanistan cost $ Trillions and thousands of deaths with little benefit for the US. Terrorist groups such as the Talaban, Alqeida, Al Shabaab, Boko Haram and ISIS formed and exist throughout the world. Terrorists form small, evolving groups or cells scattered around the world. As such, they should be fought when they pose a real national threat. They should be attacked with surgical strikes using Special Forces, targeted bombs and missiles, drone strikes, etc., when warranted given accurate definitive intelligence.

NAMING TERRORISM

The Obama administration tries to avoid use of the term "radical Islamic terrorists"as too insulting to the Islamic religion. Barbaric Sharia Law is practiced and imposed by terrorists. Sharia law abuses and degrades women and minorities and requires the killing 0f nonbelievers (infidels). A better way of naming such believers would be Sharia as; "Sharia State" instead of Islamic State, "Sharia Jihadist" or "Radical Sharia Terrorists". Moderate Muslims can correctly identify the Radical Muslims as Sharia Muslims. By correctly identifying terrorists with their practiced, Sharia law, insults to Islam and Muslims are avoided and terrorist's guiding ideology is revealed.

CONCEALED WEAPONS CARRY

A CRIME & TERRORISM DEFENSE

The best defense against crime and mass random or terrorist shootings is a populace with a significant number carrying concealed weapons.

Having the ability to defend against a criminal act or mass shooting in a home or public place is justifiable and easily understood. The police can seldom respond immediately while such crimes are being committed. So an ability to defend in real-time is clearly a good idea.

Mass shootings by a deranged individual or a few terrorists, can kill many helpless people before police can arrive. The presence of concealed carry defenders in mass shooting situations become critical to provide immediate efforts to stop the shooters and minimize loss of life.

The fact that there may be concealed weapon carriers in a crowd is a major deterrent to would be criminals or terrorists. Mass shootings occur in **gun free zones** because they know there will be little defense to their attacks in such soft target places. There will also likely be time to do damage before police are likely to arrive.

Signs denoting a **gun free zone** represent an unwise effort to protect against the use of guns in such areas. Responsible, trained, gun owners should be encouraged to provide a source of protection in all establishments. The danger from them is insignificant compared to the potential protection they can provide to crime or terrorist attacks. **Gun free zone** signs attract crime and terrorists as soft targets and should not be used.

Societies should encourage trained, responsible gun ownership, an important 2nd Amendment right. Concealed weapon carrying should also be promoted. Where this is done, crime rates are significantly lower. In past mass shootings, the presence of persons carrying concealed weapons would likely have saved many lives.

THE ROLE OF POLITICAL PARTIES

Theodore Roosevelt had this to say about political parties in his day:

"The old parties are husks, with no real soul within either, divided on artificial lines, boss-ridden and privilege-controlled, each a jumble of incongruous elements, and neither daring to speak out wisely and fearlessly on what should be said on the vital issues of the day."

This could be descriptive of the Republican and Democratic parties today. Both of these parties are focused on gaining control of the Federal Government and the enormous budget and power that comes with it. Both parties have increased the size of the Federal Government when in control and show no sign of change. . Enormous omnibus spending authorization extension bills are passed to keep government operating when budgets are not approved.

$ Trillion / Tens of $Billion budget deficits have been routinely accepted. The pursuit of government power has corrupted both parties. The two parties differ little in this respect except that the Democrats tend to expand government with more domestic spending, while the Republicans favor policies that support smaller government, business and military expenditures.

Both parties accept and are influenced by extensive funding from lobbyists and corporate and military industry interests.

Republicans promoted an image of fiscal conservatism favoring lower taxes and reduction of government functions. This image was destroyed in the 2006 election by their abandonment of fiscal responsibility. When the Republicans came to control the Presidency and the legislative branches with majorities, access to all that money and power turned them into bigger spenders than the Democrats.

The Iraq and Afghanistan wars were unfunded. President Bush added to the problem by never vetoing any Republican spending bill thereby allowing unprecedented deficits to be created. They further damaged their image with the deficit funded Medicare Drug program and the first of the TARP bank bailouts and enormous federal debt increases.

When the Republicans succumbed to these attractions, they lost their reputation as the party of constitutional small government and low taxes and thereby they discouraged the Conservative faithful. Republicans did not change government, government changed the party. The question for the Republicans now is, can they reestablish their previous reputation in a better, believable way?

THE LIBERTARIAN PARTY

The most significant 3rd party in the nation is the Libertarian Party. They run candidates for local, state and Federal offices. But their success has been very limited to a few state and federal victories. They propose a very limited role for governments that protects free exchange and prevents illegal actions. They did receive 13 million votes in the 2006 elections. Rand and Ron Paul, the current strong proponents of Libertarian principles have a dedicated and significant following. However Libertarian Party appeal is not broad enough to have major national or state impacts.

Recognizing problems with political parties, Fredrick Bastiat said this: *"I have taken the decision that, whatever happens, I will not be a Party man."*

Some suggest that, in order to get the Federal Senators and Representatives to clearly recognize that the people are clearly alarmed by the expansion of the Federal Government and the enormous debts being created, all incumbents should be voted out of office with no regard to party affiliation. This would definitely deliver the message frustration and desired change. It may be an alternative to conservative third party support which often simply dilutes Republican support and causes Democrats to be elected.

What must be accomplished in our society today is a general, public re-evaluation and re-assessment of the original system of checks and balances, with special consideration being given to why they failed and how they or others which are more effective can be re-established and effectively maintained. A necessary preliminary to such actions would be the accomplishment of a re-awakening of the people to the vital importance of such disciplines in any system of government and to the dangers inherent in any system where they do not exist.

In Article 15 of the Virginia Declaration of Rights, which was drafted by George Mason and adopted in 1776, appears this statement:

*"No free government or the blessings of liberty can be preserved to any people but by firm adherence to justice, moderation, temperance, frugality, and virtue and by **frequent recurrence to fundamental principles.**"* **The time for "recurrence" is long overdue.**

What is clear is that if the Republican Party continues in its disregard to constitutional principles and support of fiscally irresponsible policies it will become an irrelevant party and will be replaced with a new one based on Independent Constitutional principles. **Unfortunately this may only develop after a national debt driven insolvency crises occurs.**

All of the budget plans currently proposed by the Democrats or Republicans only address reducing budget deficits (the amount over a balanced budget) adding annually to the national debt.. These plans only slow the amount of budget growth. They propose reducing the deficit over a 10 year period. No meaningful cuts are made now.

These plans require that future legislators must do the actual cutting. A very dubious assumption.

None of the current plans actually reduce the $18+ Trillion current national debt. In fact, even if the proposed cuts are actually done over the 10 year period, $7 – 8 Trillion more will likely be added to the national debt increasing it to over $20 Trillion because budgets will not be balanced during this period with current proposed plans. The current $18+ Trillion national debt is larger than all the European economies combined. How long can this go on? How can our children deal with these massive generational debt burdens?

If the Federal Debt is ever to be reduced, the first requirement is to balance the Federal Budget by eliminating the annual deficits. What is the deficit? It is the amount by which the Federal Government outlays exceeds its total income for a fiscal year. Such deficits are added to the accumulating national debt.

Recent US Federal Deficits

Obama Deficits *Billions*	*Bush Deficits* *Billions*
FY 2015: $439	
FY 2014: $432	
FY 2013: $680	FY 2009: $1,413
FY 2012: $1,089	
FY 2011: $1,270	FY 2008: $459
FY 2010: $1,293	FY 2007: $161

The National Debt will continue to grow as long as deficits continue to add to it. So the key question is, how can the Federal Budget be balanced and the national debt reduced? It will require elimination or reduction of many of the current operations of the Federal Government. In many cases, the operations may be returned to the States to assume their correct role in these operations. **A recurrence to Constitutional Principles will be required.**

National debt default and insolvency will occur when the interest on the national debt seriously erodes the funds available to meet national budgetary requirements.

The low current interest rates disguise the debt interest problem that rising interest rates will bring.The Federal Reserve has been providing 0% borrowing rates for years to stimulate a stagnant economy and now has begun increasing these rates to more normal levels.

Interest rates on U.S. bonds are currently low, but that doesn't mean the country's future interest payments on the national debt will be. The government will pay out more than $5 trillion in interest payments over the next decade, according to the latest projections from the Congressional Budget Office.

Over the decade, more than 14% of *all revenue* the government is projected to collect will be paid out in interest payments. That's a lot of money that cannot be used on the country's other priorities. Indeed, between 2013 and 2022, estimated interest costs will be:

Higher than Medicaid spending;

Equal to half of Social Security spending;

More than what is spent on all of Defense.

The estimated interest costs assume a fairly steady and moderate increase in rates over the decade.

The CBO assumes that the yield on the 10-year Treasury will rise from an estimated current 2.3% to 5% by the end of the decade; and the yield on the 3-month T-bill will increase from 0.1% to 3.8% during the same time.

With the Federal Reserve continuing "Quantitative Easing", buying bonds and printing money, to fund continuing debt this fiat money is bound to eventually cause inflation. The Fed will then increase interest rates to combat inflation. Interest payments are immediate demands on the Federal Budget thereby increasing deficits adding to the National Debt or drastically cutting into other spending.

These interest payment potentials represent the greatest national security danger leading to National Debt default and insolvency.

The best potential for surviving these debt crises is by supporting powerful growth of the national economy. This must be stimulated by tax incentive and limiting regulation policies that will generate such expansion.

LIFE CHANGING POTENTIALS

Increasing Energy production, computing, Artificial Intelligence, nano and cell technology and new materials are just some of the developments that have the potentials to change the world as we know it at an exponential, unpredictable rate. It is conceivable that developments such as this will change economies and life in ways that cannot be predicted.They will contribute to the economic growth necessary to correct the national debt crises,

ENERGY ECONOMIC POTENTIALS

The greatest growth potential exists in positive expansion of energy resources. The US has the potential to become energy independent and energy rich if national policies and incentives focus on such resources. Oil, natural gas, coal, nuclear must all be supported and promoted. Solar and wind power generation can also be supported as they develop and becomes economically competitive.

Natural gas is an efficient energy source and the cleanest-burning fossil fuel. Natural gas extracted from dense shale rock formations has become the fastest-growing source of gas in the United States. Energy companies have combined two established technologies—hydraulic fracturing and horizontal drilling to successfully unlock energy resources.

The U.S. Energy Information Administration (EIA) estimates the United States possesses more than 2,500 Trillion cubic feet of technically recoverable natural gas resources, of which 33 percent is held in shale rock formations. Natural gas from shale has grown to 25 percent of U.S. gas production in just a decade and will be 50 percent by 2035, according to the EIA. Developing this resource can help enhance energy security and strengthen economies. As the distribution infrastructure for delivery and wide scale use of this energy resource in transportation is accomplished, the economy will benefit enormously.

An energy rich and independent US will not only contribute to the economic growth necessary to correct its fiscal debt crises, it will also allow reduced terrorist dangers. The US will no longer be threatened by the instability and hostility of mid-east petroleum suppliers.

THE EFFECTS OF INCREASING COMPUTER POWER

Another force that will powerfully strengthen and stimulate the economy is the continuing acceleration of the speed and power of computers. Gordon Moore, a CEO of the Intel Corporation manufacturer of computer and memory chips defined the nature of the evolution of computer power.

Moore's law *is the observation that "over the history of computing hardware, the number of transistors on integrated circuits doubles approximately every two years".*

This means that computers decrease in size and double in speed and memory capacity every 2 years. What is amazing is that this improvement in computer power is likely to continue for the foreseeable future.

The influence of this multiplying computer power has the potential to accelerate the productivity and expansion of the US economy as well as world inter-connectivity. It is impossible to accurately predict what or how this will influence this nation and the world. But surely it will have a powerful effect on society and economic potentials. As computing power proliferates and is integrated into products, more control and intelligence increases their value.

Robotics and 3D printing of products and parts will become more capable increasing accuracy, speed and productivity thereby vastly improving manufacturing efficiencies. As computing power is further integrated into transportation, vehicles and roads, safety and efficiencies will be greatly improved.

Position sensing systems combined with the increasing cability of self generated robotic application programming present potentials for rapid proliferation of job automation. Any job with predictable, repetitive steps and outcome will be a candidate for computer automation. This will likely result in enormous productivity improvement. Which will also have significant impact on jobs, career paths and skill development.

Nano-technology is the manipulation of matter on an atomic and molecular scale. Generally, nano-technology works with materials, devices, and other structures with at least one dimension sized from 1 to 100 nano-meters. Quantum mechanical effects are important at this quantum-realm scale. With a variety of potential applications, nano-technology is a key technology for the future.

Graphene is a new wonder material. It's the thinnest electronic material ever invented, consisting of a layer of carbon atoms just a single atom thick. The atoms are arranged in a hexagonal pattern. It weighs almost nothing, coming in at only 0.77 grams for a square meter.

Graphene is 100 times stronger than steel of the same thickness. It conducts both heat and electricity better than copper, and has outstanding optical and mechanical properties. Initially this will mean that graphene is used to help improve the performance and efficiency of current materials and substances. In the future it will also be developed with other two-dimensional (2D) crystals to create some even more amazing compounds.

As nano-technology and micro computing is incorporated with new materials, many careers and products will evolve in life changing ways that are incomprehensible today.

PART VIII

THE GREATEST NEED

The suggested Federal Limit Amendment is an example of a corrective measure that could be taken. It is presented to illustrate the principles discussed. It could be done to perform the function of "**Recurrence to Fundamental Principles**" which is essential to the maintenance of a free society. If something like it cannot be reasonably accomplished in today's political climate, it may be more of a reactionary kind of action that would be more feasible after occurrence of national fiscal insolvency.

Examinations and thought which will find ways to effectively perform '"recurrence to constitutional principle" represents the greatest lack in the present day American political society. Even disciplines such as Pay-Go policies which require that every new expenditure must be funded from other parts of the budget or the Presidential Line Veto which would allow the President to eliminate line item spending form bills that he signs are not used.

Term limits for representatives would also improve government control attitudes by removing incentives for career politicians. Also adding "sunset provisions" to laws to force periodic review and rejustification of need would strengthen congressional oversight and recurrence to principle but are seldom included in legislation.

Most prevailing political and governmental thought is polarized with either the "progressive (liberal) greater government" or "conservative limited government" philosophies. The major choices are between two extremes. We must stop the wild oscillations between these extremes. Both extremes have serious faults that are clearly recognizable. Creative minds that can fill the vacuum in between these extremes represent this nation's greatest need.

Liberals (now known as Progressives) have been extremely effective in promoting positive images for their causes in the public's mind. For example, all government spending is now called "investment". This positive image has been mainly accomplished because their causes have been responsive to problems.

They are really no more humane people than conservatives. Liberals are simply liberal in their willingness to use governmental funds and force to solve problems. For this they are applauded by those who receive the help; the bureaucrats, and politicians who administer the services, a supportive media and a gullible taker citizenry.

They irresponsibly advocate "greater government" as the panacea for all social ills with no regard for potential dangers inherent in the fiscal dangers they turn loose. Solve the problems, they cry. The end would justify the means. Disregard that the funding needed sources for such programs are ignored or irresponsibly provided by adding to debt.

Problems must be solved but badly conceived and deficit funded and poorly administered solutions can have broader and more terrible effects than the problems themselves. Do liberals really deserve the positive image they enjoy? Definitely not, for they have let their compassion run away with, their common sense.

They have forgotten George Washington's admonition that government can also be a "fearful master".

Libertarian principles, except for civil liberties, have been left to the conservatives for advocacy and defense. Conservative negativism has too often served to hide the lights of liberty under clouds of un-constructive governmental criticism, problematic disregard, paranoid anti-communism and anti-terrorism war.

If Constitutional principles are to be effective in America, they must be placed in a new context of governmental philosophy that stresses the positive aspects of compassion and sensitivity to problems. This philosophy must advocate principles that foster an effective, responsive and freedom supporting government through processes of <u>automatic</u> adjustment and functional leveling that need not rely on a consistent critical citizenry for their operation.

This is not only a challenge for those of a conservative or libertarian mind. It is a challenge for all who believe in Constitutional government and the American dream of freedom for the individual.

It is probably the most important question facing America today and it is especially significant for the younger generation.

It may well be that the young people sense that the root principles of our society no longer have validity and, in the questioning manner of youth, they are rebelling against the old concepts of government. They correctly believe that the enormous debts that they will have to deal with in their generation will drastically limit their potential for success.

Few believe that Social Security will be available for them. Their searching is disorganized and they have no clear goals in mind. It is here submitted that a goal worthy of all possible efforts would be the invention and creation of Constitutional principles that provide effective, responsive government functioning in a society that retains maximum freedom for the individual.

American principles of limited government, freedom and free markets have created the greatest, most successful nation in the history of the world. With effective recurrence to constitutional government that is effective and responsive, an even better, shining example of an ideal society can be provided to the world.

Rather than promoting such ideal society's principles through force and ineffective nation building campaigns, let other societies be persuaded by an excellent, successful American example.

We are at a medieval stage in terms of intelligent use and control of government in society. Our ability to design and implement new, functional systems of governmental control will determine whether we now move into a dark age of smothering, fiscal bankruptcy, irresponsible socialistic over government, dependency and an eventual end to the "American dream of freedom".

Can we evaluate the past and from this evaluation reform the principles of freedom and government thereby giving a new vitality and concern to American politics? Creative minds that can provide answers to fill the vacuum between right and left extremism constitute this nation's greatest present need. Hopefully, such a need cannot go unfulfilled.

Is mankind always to be manipulated and ultimately overwhelmed by governmental processes? This question is especially pertinent for Americans today. Certainly the evidence of history relating to the pattern of social governmental evolution and destruction must eventually move mankind to develop effective control systems. For America, the question is valid and, as yet, unanswered. Will we be capable of breaking the cycle or will we remain apathetic and insensitive and follow it to its deadening socialistic/dependent end or worse?

Man, as a creative, intelligent being, certainly has the capacity to devise functional, effective methods of government. This is clearly proven in any examination of the myriad governmental forms and innovations created through history.

The American Constitution is an example of a giant step taken toward concepts of freedom, of balanced, ideal, limited government. So it would seem very realistic that an effort could be made again based on our recent experiences and all the examples of history. **A "recurrence to principles" is not only possible, it is essential for survival**.

Our current path of fiscal irresponsibility which is leading to a National Debt that is greater than our Annual Gross Domestic Product and future spending projections that could actually lead to national Insolvency. As $ devaluation and interest rates rise, the need to pay these rates required to sustain the massive national debt will drastically impact the nation's ability to meet its required expenditures.

Continuing down this path, Atlas America will have to shrug off the weight of the world. It will have no choice.

Our ancestors passed on the principles of liberty relatively intact to us. The greatest damages to these principles have been done with in the past forty years. It is probably not yet too late for a **"recurrence to fundamental principles"**, a **Return To Constitutional Federal Government.** It may be too late before very long.

What will we pass on to our grandchildren; massive, uncontrollable government and unsustainable national debts? Will this still be a nation founded on Constitutional principles of effective government that work in a free society? Will Abraham Lincoln's description of America having "Government of the people, by the people and for the people" still apply? With awareness, concern and action it can be so.

Who is B. J. Galt?

The author; B. J. Galt is the pseudonym of a retired Computer System Engineer. He has published three books defining how end users can be designers of major applications. He originated the design of a computer software system which was responsible for >$3 Billion in system sales for a major corporation.

This book describes the author's reflections, concerns and recommendations based on over 40 years of observance of large, corporate bureaucracy and political history. As a past Conservative and Republican, he now describes himself as a "Constitutional Independent".

The book represents his evolved, current, political perspectives. It suggests solutions and initiatives to accomplish a **"recurrence to constitutional principles"** thereby returning Constitutional powers to the states and providing for a Federal Government that is fiscally sound, effective in its operations and responsive to the nation's needs while restoring liberty to the individual, dignity to the legislature and purpose to the ballot box.

PUBLISHING

For printed copies of this book:

https://www.createspace.com

Atlas America

Title ID: 4064790

Also on Kindle & at Amazon Books

ISBN-13 978-1481049306

ISBN-10 1481049305

Email request a Free book PDF from

B. J. Galt Email: bjongalt@gmail.com

Atlas America

Summary Presentation

ATLAS AMERICA
On Point

Will Atlas Shrug?

A State Ratified Federal Limit Amendment, Need A 3rd Party? Constitutional Federal Government

By B. J. Galt

American Success

America represents a unique, shining example in government. Its success is the envy of people all over the world. World economies depend on US success.

US GDP is > China, Japan, UK, Germany combined.

Many countries depend on America for economic,   charitable and military support.

America is truly Atlas to the World!

When faced with a $18+Trillion, national debt; Will Atlas Shrug?

Military Support

Many countries depend on America for military and economic support.

Where in the world is our Military?

On 700+ bases in 135 nations

The 2015 Military Budget was $610 Billion excluding Iraq and Afghanistan war costs.

The United States military budget accounts for 40% of the world's military spending.

America is Atlas to the world

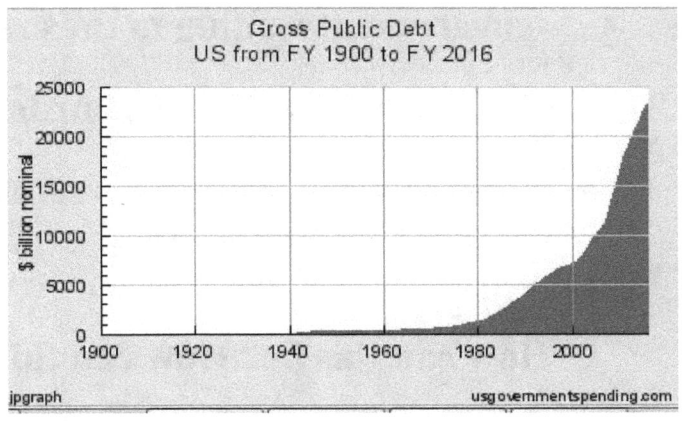

The 2015 Federal debt is $18+ Trillion. Continuing Deficit spending adds to the debt every year. Insolvency due to required debt interest payments is a real possibility.

Loss Of Government Control

The danger for America is that the people lose control of their government leading to the creation of excessive, Inefficient, burdensome, character-crushing government dependence.

How can this be? How can this great people, possessed of such literacy and the best communications that technology can provide be in danger losing control of their government? The government has become too large to be effectively controlled through elected representatives.

Republican Spending

President Bush added to the problem by never vetoing any Republican spending bill.

He authorized the Iraq and Afghanistan wars, the Part D Medication program, the Economic Stimulus Act of 2008 and the TARP bank bailout, all without budgetary funding, thereby allowing unprecedented deficits to be created.

The Republicans lost their ideals as a party of small constitutional government and low taxes.

Democrat Spending

In the first years of the Obama administration, using congressional majorities and the Presidency, the $800 Billion American Recovery and Reinvestment Act of 2009 was passed without funding to stimulate the economy.

This added to the Federal Deficit in that year.   It did little to eliminate the recession. It did   increase federal and state spending.

The Affordable Care Act

The Obama administration and
Democrat congressional majority
passed the 2500 page Affordable
Care Act (Obama Care) without
any Republican support.
This has future implications of
massive increases in taxes,
federal controls, bureaucracies
and related health costs.

Unbalanced Budget Proposals

Democrat or Republican budget plans only reduce the amount of budget growth, not current spending. Future legislators must do the actual cutting.

None of the plans reduce the $18+ Trillion current national debt. Over the next 10 year period, $7 – 8 Trillion will be added to the debt. How Long before funding realities will force insolvency?

How will our children deal with these generational debt burdens?

Recent US Federal Deficits

Obama Deficits $ Billions	Bush Deficits $ Billions
FY 2015: $439	
FY 2014: $432	
FY 2013: $680	
FY 2012: $1,089	
FY 2011: $1,270	FY 2009: $1,413
FY 2010: $1,293	FY 2008: $459
	FY 2007: $161

The Peter Principle

The Peter Principle states; "In a bureaucracy, everyone tends to rise to their level of incompetence, then they are no longer promoted. In time, every post tends to be occupied by an incompetent employee."

This principle and problem is very true in government as well as the private   sector . Federal employee protective unions make this problem even greater.

A Limit To Size?

"To the size of a state there is a limit, as there is to plants, animals and implements, for they can not retain their facility when they are too large."

Aristotle

A Tipping Point

The critical point is when the number of people living on government entitlements passes 50% and can control future elections.

Today, 45% of US citizens pay no income taxes.

The Democratic party has majority support from all minorities, welfare recipients, unions, and government workers making it difficult for anyone to propose any reduction in government spending or programs.

Constitutional Road Blocks

The Constitution of the United States is unique among the constitutions of the world in the way it restricts the powers of the Federal Government with checks and balances.

Its allowed powers are specifically listed in the 10th Amendment which then states:

"The powers not delegated to the United States by the Constitution, nor prohibited by it to the States, are reserved to the States respectively, or to the people."

Dollar Purchasing Power

Devaluation

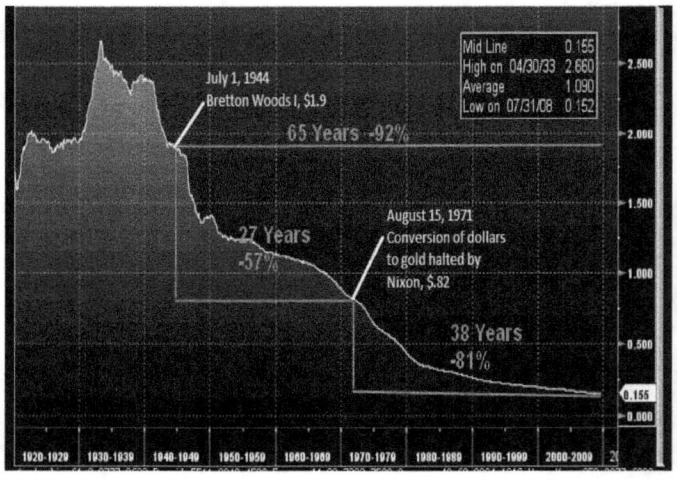

This chart shows $ devaluation up to the year 2000. How much more has the Federal Reserve devalued the dollar with Quantitative Easing (printing money) since then?

Physical Dimensions Of Money

Not too long ago, $1 Billion ($ One Thousand Million) was the maximum sum used to describe most government spending.

Even $ One Billion is not clearly understood by most people.

$1 Billion = A stack of $1 bills 75 Miles high.

$1 Trillion = One Thousand Billions.

$1 BILLION in ½" packages of $10,000 of $100 bills

$1 Trillion in ½" packages

Of $10,000 of $100 bills

Billions And Trillions

The next time you hear politicians speak of Billion and Trillion dollar budgets and expenditures, consider the physical dimensions of the money they are proposing to spend.

When a politician says he is proposing to spend $1 Billion for a project, ask him if it is worth 1,000 Million Dollars?
See if his answer shows that he really appreciates what a Billion Dollars truly represents.

Deficit And Debt Problems

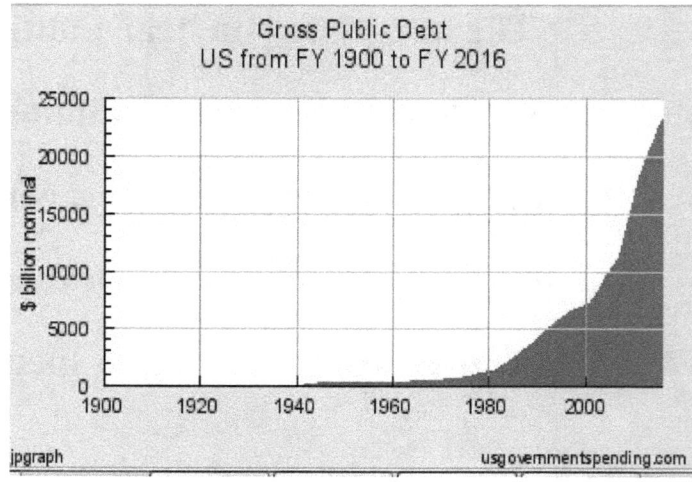

The 2015 Federal debt is $18+ Trillion. Deficit spending adds to the debt every year. Insolvency due to growing debt interest payments is a real possibility.

Neither party proposes balanced budgets. What will we pass on to our grandchildren; unfillable program promises, uncontrollable government and unsustainable national debts?

Interest Payment Danger

Debt interest costs which must paid from current budgets will be:
Higher than Medicaid spending,
Equal to half of Social Security spending.
Close to what is spent on all of Defense

Driven by rising % rates to fight inflation, debt interest payment requirements represent the greatest danger leading to national insolvency.

How To Survive

To Eliminate deficits and reduce the debt to avoid national insolvency:

+Eliminate unconstitutional federal spending.

+Promote powerful growth of the national economy; Energy production, Computing Power, Nano & Graphene technology, etc.

+Support Tax reform and regulation policies that will generate economic expansion.

<u>**Current Constitutional Checks and Balances are inadequate to affect needed change. Consider:**</u>

A FEDERAL LIMIT AMENDMENT

The total annual expenditures of the Federal Government of the United States shall not exceed a limit established at the time of ratification of this amendment except as may be authorized at any time for periods of up to twelve months by at least fifty one percent of the State Legislatures. After ratification of this amendment, all income of the Federal Government of the United States in excess of the established expenditure limit shall be disbursed to the States on the basis of population or shall be used to reduce the national debt.

States Rights

The states, in initial agreement, designed, created and ratified the Constitution of the United States. Ultimately, the states must agree that the Federal government conforms to the requirements of the US Constitution.

If the Federal Government significantly deviates from the Constitution, Article 5 defines the right of states to propose and ratify amendments as needed; "Ammendment ratification by ¾ of the States or by conventions."

Basic Disciplines Created

1. Control of the size and growth of The Federal Government through a constitutional Federal Budget limit.

2. Debt reduction or dispersion of excess federal funds to states in a manner that is nationally equitable and not subject to federal political influence.

3. Federal competition for available funds within the budget limit will increase program oversight, rejustification and the reduction and elimination of unnecessary and duplicate functions.

More Disciplines

4. State competition for available funds would add an additional check and balance effect to the Federal Government.

5. The Constitutional Congressional Power to declare war would be reinforced.

The Vietnam, Iraq and Afghanistan wars would likely not have been authorized and funded with this amendment in effect.

6. States rights and constitutional federalism would be strengthened.

This fact would provide a strong incentive for states to use their constitutional right to ratify a Federal Limit Amendment.

War On Terror

The term "War On Terror" is a good example of over exaggeration of a threat to justify defense spending. A "War On Terror" will likely never see a definable end. Terror is a reaction and terrorism is a tactic not a nation state to be attacked. One cannot wage war on a reaction or tactic to any satisfactory conclusion.

Naming Terror

In the "War On Terror", The Obama administration avoids use of the term "radical Islamic terrorists"as insulting to the Islamic religion. Barbaric Sharia Law is practiced and imposed by terrorists. Sharia law abuses and degrades women, minorities and kills Muslim nonbelievers. Instead, name them; "Sharia State" instead of Islamic State, "Sharia Jihadist" or "Radical Sharia Terrorists". Moderate Muslims can identify the Radical Muslims as Sharia Muslims. Then insults to Islam / Muslims are avoided and terrorist's guiding ideology is revealed.

Concealed Weapons Carry
A Crime and Terrorism
Attack Defense

The best defense against crime and mass shootings is a populace with a significant number carrying concealed weapons. The police seldom respond while such crimes are being committed. The ability to defend in real-time is critical . Concealed carry defenders in mass shooting situations become critical to provide immediate efforts to stop the shooters and minimize loss of life.

Other Disciplines Possible

+Pay Go policies require every new, proposed spending must be funded.

+A Presidential Line Veto allows the President to eliminate line item spending from bills.

+Term Limits for Representatives removing incentives for career politicians.

+Add Sunset Provisions to existing and new laws to force periodic review and rejustification

Other Disciplines Possible

+Pass a law: Any member of congress voting for a budget with a deficit of more than 3% of GDP will be ineligible for re-election.

+A Constitution Amendment: Congress shall make no law that applies to the citizens of the United States that does not apply equally to the Senators and/or Representatives; and, Congress shall make no law that applies to the Senators and/or Representatives that does not apply equally to the citizens of the United States.

Another Discipline Possible

Enforce the Mack Penny Plan:
To balance the Federal Budget in 8
years; cut 1 penny from each federal
$ spent for 6 years & cap spending at
18% of GDP beginning in the 7th
year. If congress fails to make the
cuts, the plan triggers automatic
across-the-board cuts to meet
yearly caps.

TO SURVIVE THE DEBT CRISIS

Support powerful growth of the national economy with tax incentives and by reducing government regulation.

LIFE CHANGING POTENTIALS

Increasing Energy production, computing power, Artificial Intelligence, nano and cell technology and new materials are developments that have the potentials to change the world as we know it at an exponential rate.

They will help supply the economic growth to survive the fiscal debt crises.

Energy Economic Potential

Great potential exists in expansion of energy resources. The US has the potential to become energy independent and energy rich if national policies and incentives focus on such resources.

Oil, natural gas, coal, nuclear must all be supported and promoted. Solar and wind power generation Alternatives can also be supported as they develop and become economically viable.

The Power Of Computing

Another force that has and will powerfully strengthen and stimulate the economy is the continuing acceleration of the speed and power of computers. Gordon Moore, a CEO of the Intel Corporation chip manufacturer stated Moore's Law:

"Over the history of computers, the number of transistors on chips doubles approximately every two years".

Moore's Law

This means that computers decrease in size and double in speed and memory capacity every 2 years. This doubling of computer power is likely to continue.

This multiplying computer power has the potential to continue to accelerate the productivity & expansion of the US economy & world interconnectivity.

Computer Power Integration

As computing power proliferates and is integrated into products, more control and intelligence will increase their value. Robotics and 3D printing of parts will become more capable increasing accuracy, speed and productivity improving Manufacturing processes.

As computing power is further integrated into transportation vehicles and roads, safety and efficiencies will be greatly improved.

NanoTechnology Potentials

Nanotechnology is the manipulation
of matter on an atomic, molecular
scale. Nanotechnology works with
materials, devices, and other
structures sized from
1 to 100 nanometers.

With a variety of potential
applications, nanotechnology is a
key technology for the future.
As micro computing is integrated
with nanotechnology, many products
will evolve in ways that are
incomprehensible today.

Grahpene A Wonder Material

Graphene is the world's new wonder material. It'sthe thinnest electronic material ever invented,consisting of a layer of carbon atoms just a singleatom thick. It weighs only 0.77 grams for a square meter.

Graphene is 100 times stronger than steel of the same thickness. It conducts both heat and electricity better than copper, and has outstanding optical and mechanical properties.

Graphene is used to improve the performanceand efficiency of current materials andsubstances.

As nano-technology & micro computing iscombined with new materials, like graphene,many new fields and products will evolve in lifechanging ways that cannot be envisioned today.

The Future?

We are at a medieval stage in terms of intelligent use and control of government in society.

Our ability to design and implement new, functional systems of government control will determine whether we now move into a dark age of smothering, fiscal bankruptcy, irresponsible, socialistic over-government and an eventual end to the "American Dream".

No Effective System?

If our founding principles with
defined checks and balances
cannot be
made to work, if our people cannot
make sound readjustments and
maintain effective control of their
government;
<u>Then there is no government
system known to mankind that will
not eventually be destroyed by its
parental society.</u>

Fulfill This Need

Can we evaluate the past and from this evaluation reform the principles of freedom and government thereby giving a new vitality and concern to American politics?

Creative minds that can provide answers to fill the vacuum between right and left extremism constitute this nation's greatest present need. Hopefully, such a need cannot go unfulfilled.

What Legacy?

What will we pass on to our grandchildren; unfillable program promises, massive, uncontrollable government and unsustainable national debts? Will this still be a nation founded on Constitutional principles of effective government in a free society? Will Abraham Lincoln's description of America having "Government of the people, by the people and for the people" still apply? With awareness, concern and action it can be so.

Who Is B. J. Galt?

This is the pseudonym of a retired Computer System Engineer. He has published three books defining how end users can be designers of major applications. He originated the design of a computer software system which was responsible for >$3 Billion in system sales for a major corporation.

This book describes the author's reflections, concerns and recommendations based on over 40 years observance of large, corporate bureaucracy and political history. As a past Conservative and Republican, he now describes himself as a "Constitutional Independent". The book represents his evolved, current, political perspectives. It suggests solutions to accomplish a "recurrence to constitutional principles".

Publishing

This summary document, "Atlas America On Point"denotes the key points made in the book;

"**Atlas America**"A State Ratified Federal Limit Amendment, Need A 3rd Party? Constitutional Federal Government"

Printed copies of this "On Point" summary & the "**Atlas America**" book are available at: Createspace.com
https://www.createspace.com/4064790

Also on Kindle & at Amazon Books

ISBN-13: 978-1481049306

ISBN-10: 1481049305

Email request a Free PDF at B. J. Galt Email: bjongalt@gmail.com